I0410643

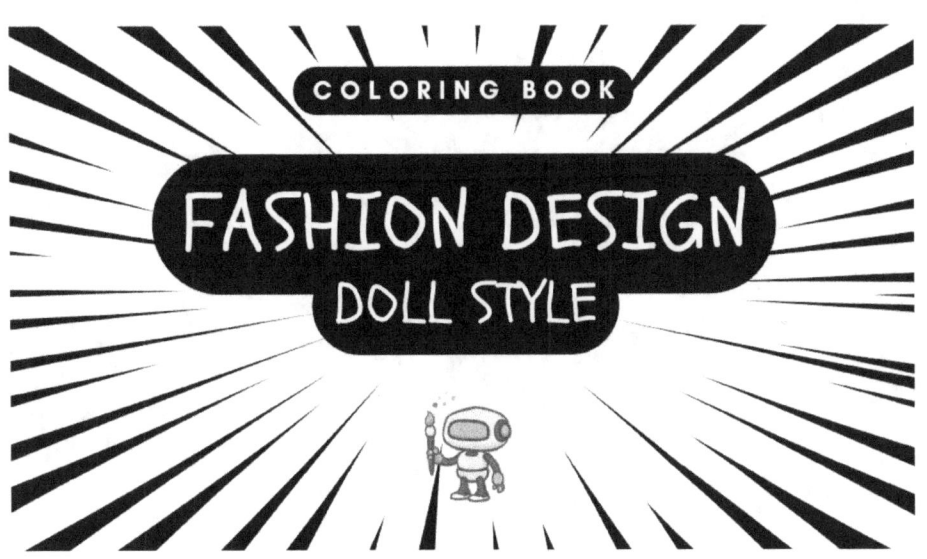

COLORING BOOK

FASHION DESIGN
DOLL STYLE

Lidia Contreras Ochando
 @liconoc

"Artificial Art" Collection
 @lilinocbooks

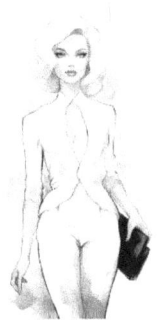

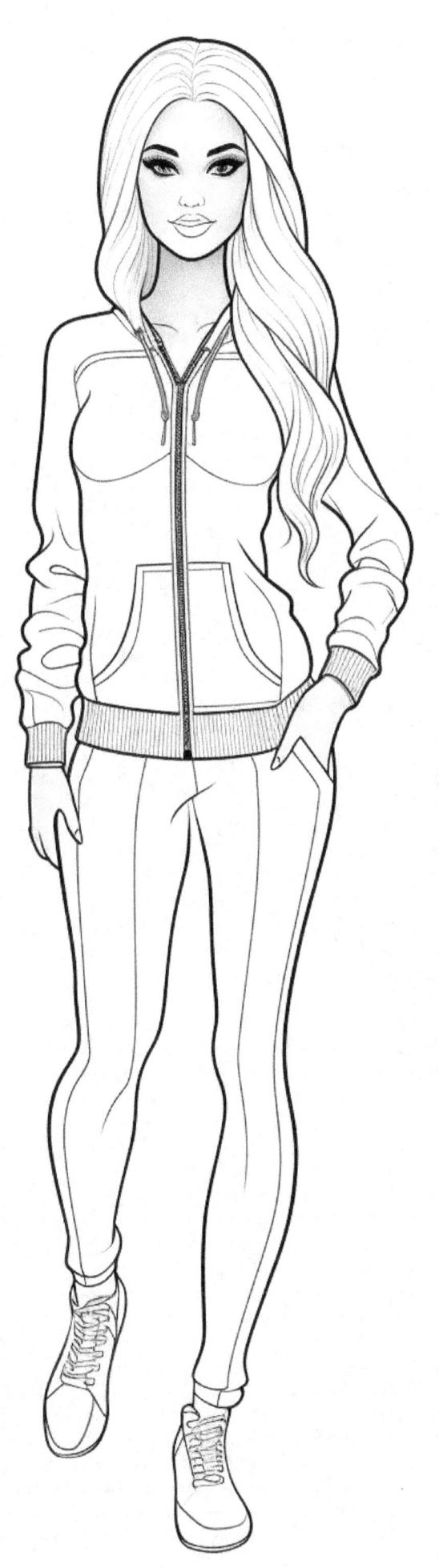

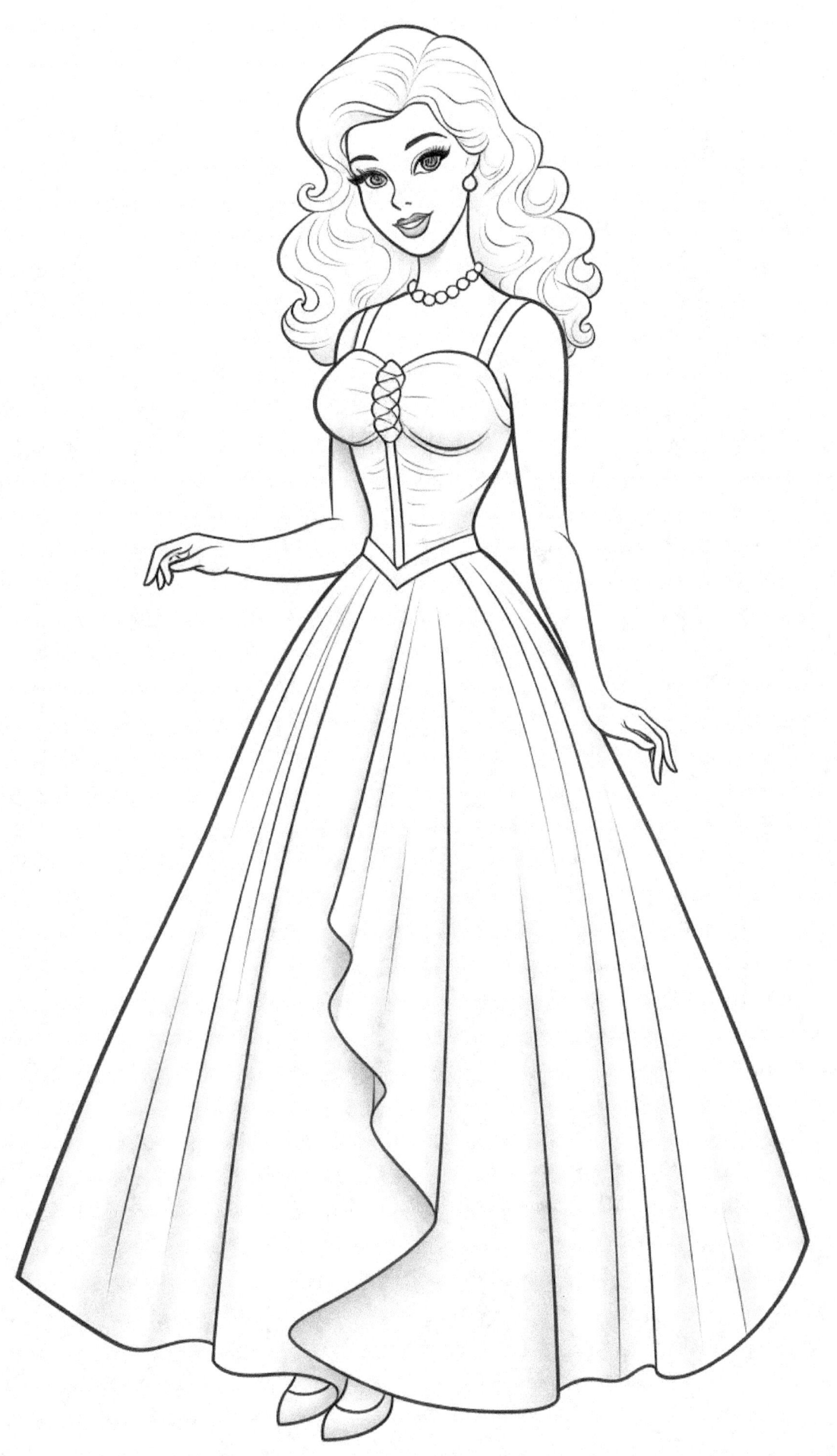

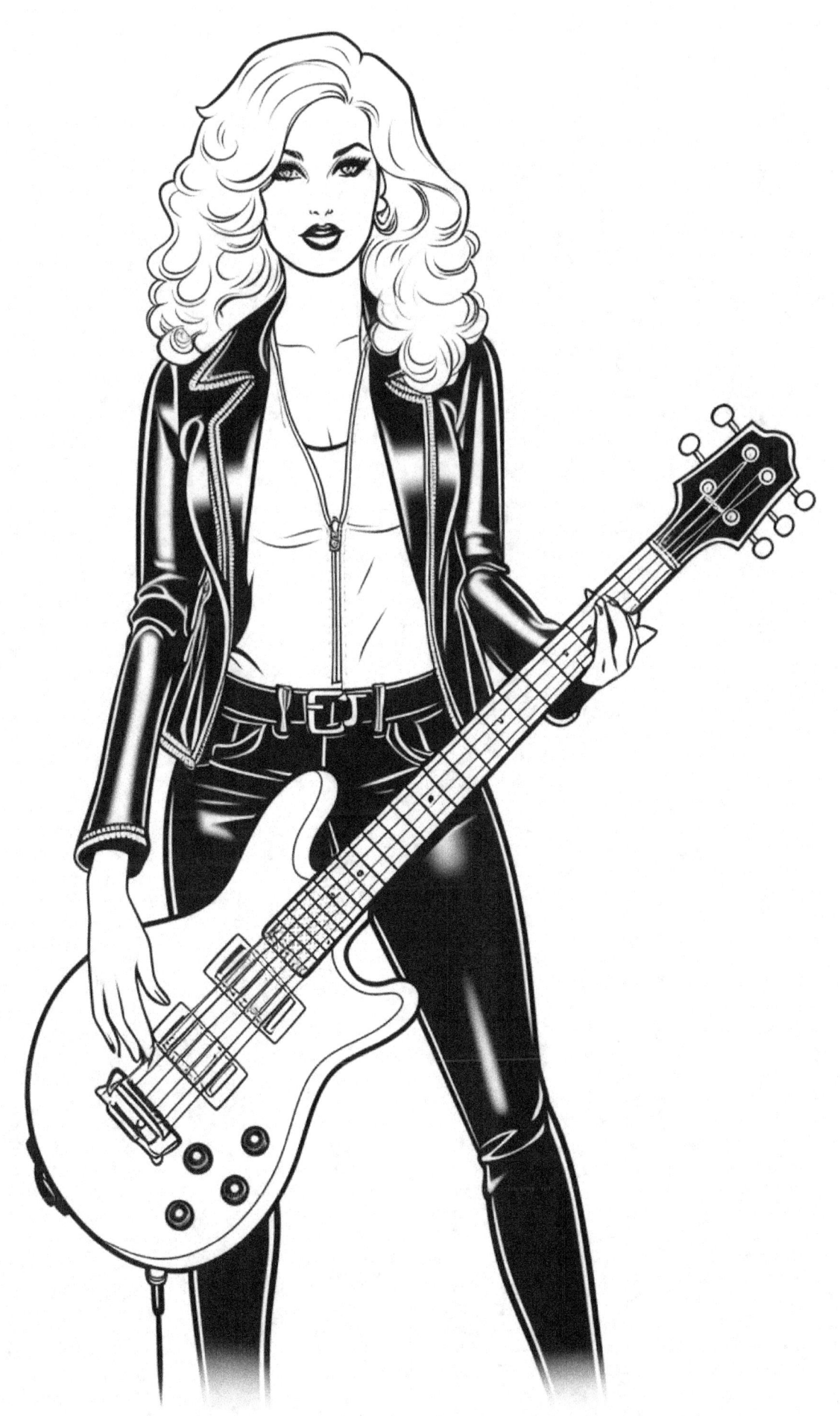

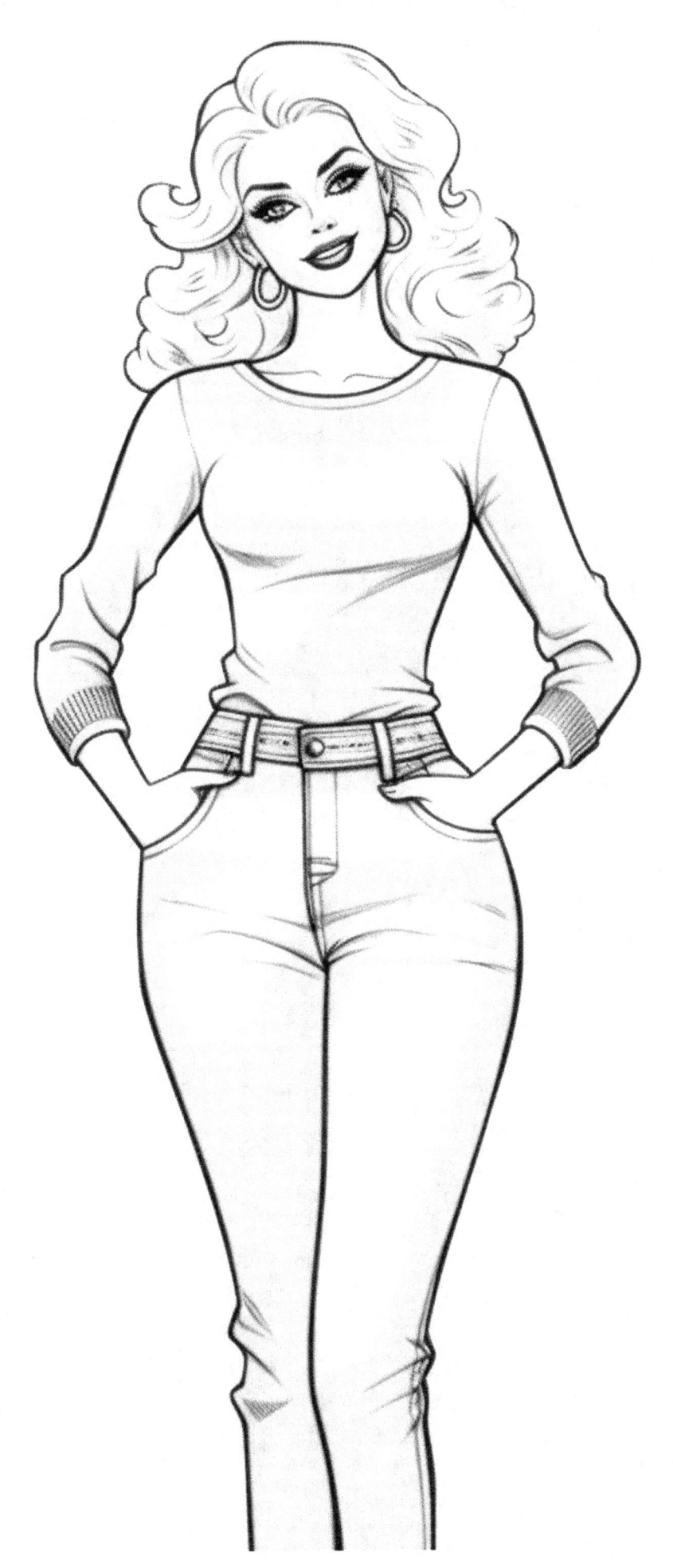

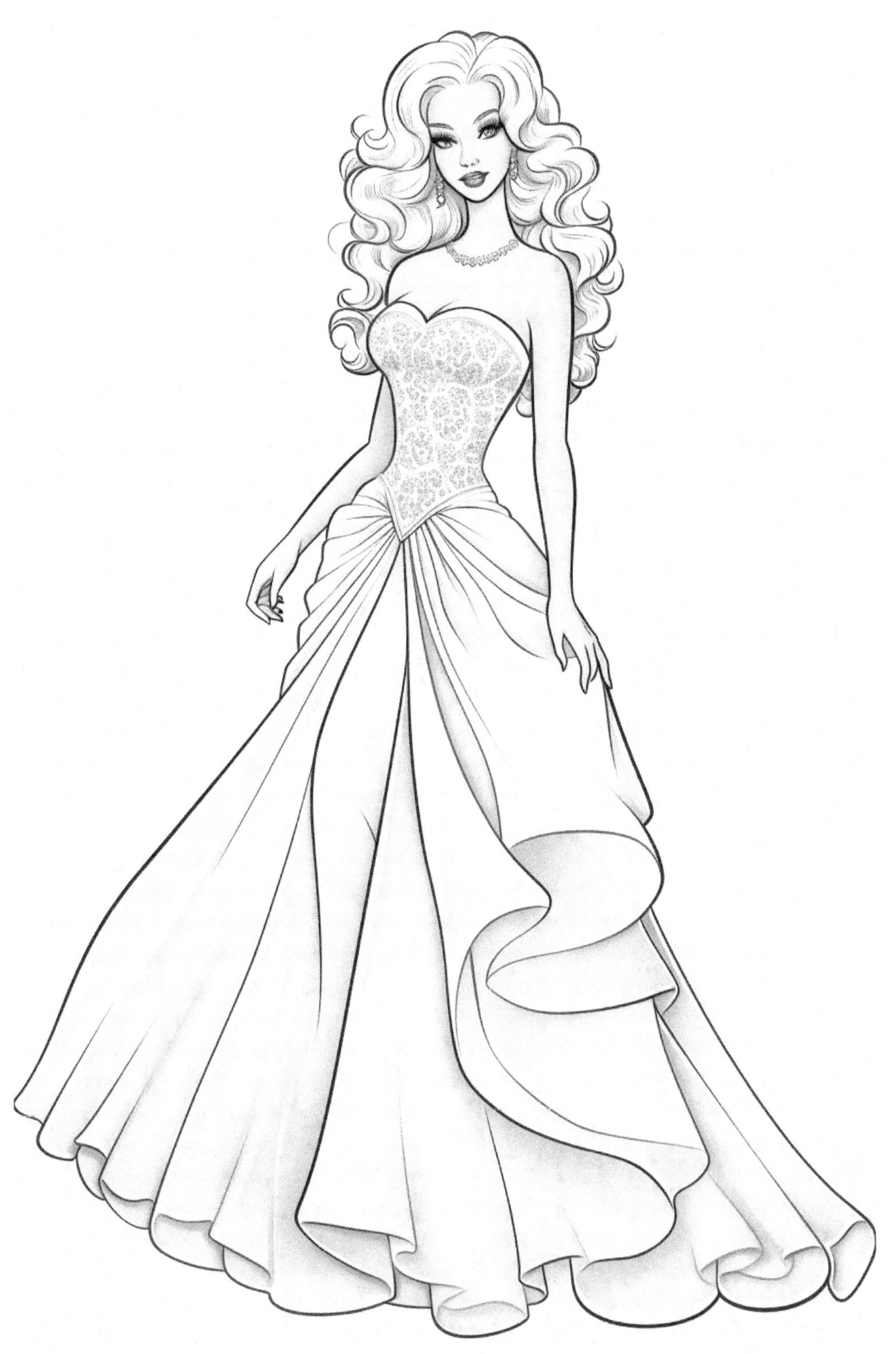

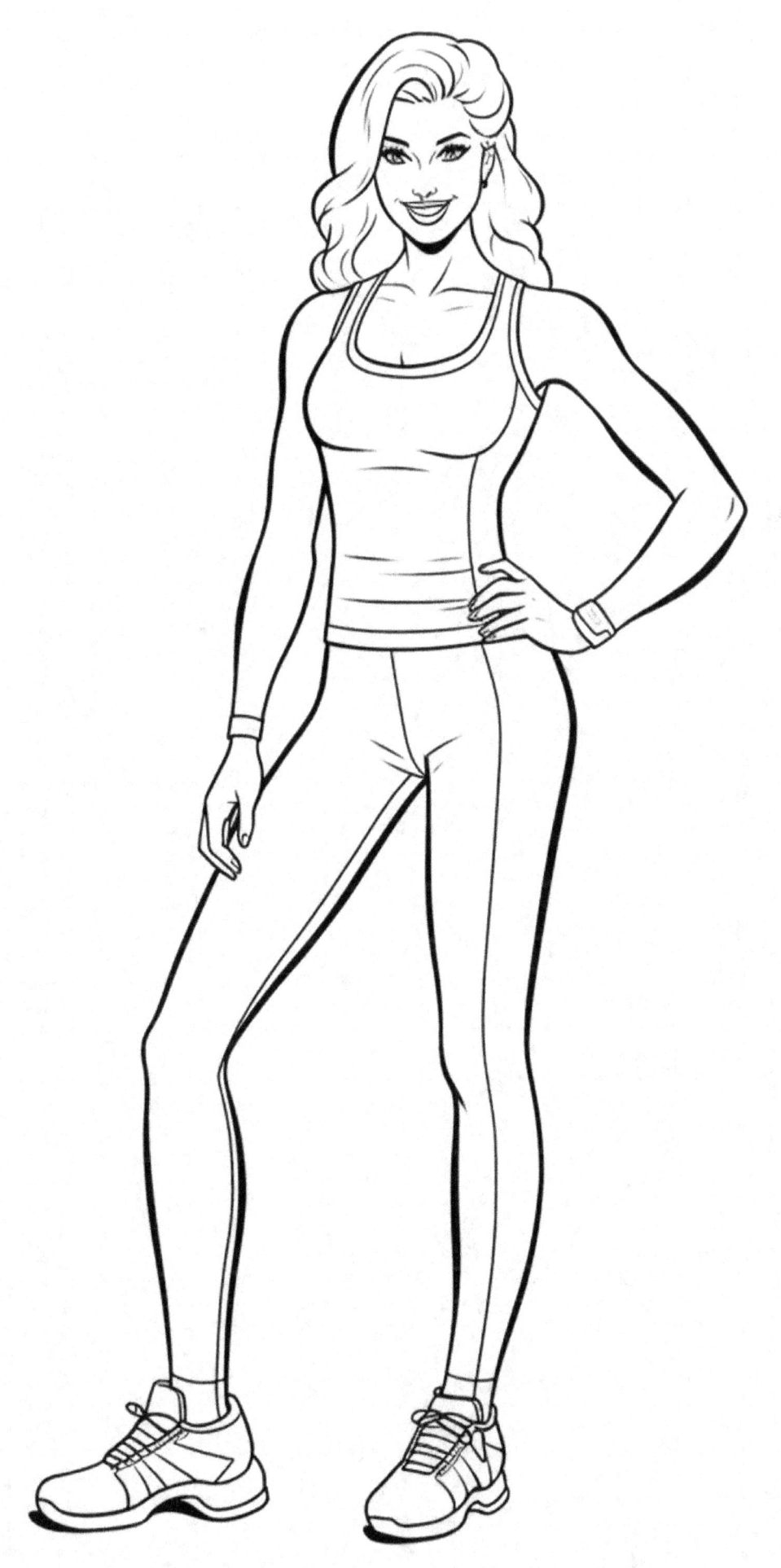

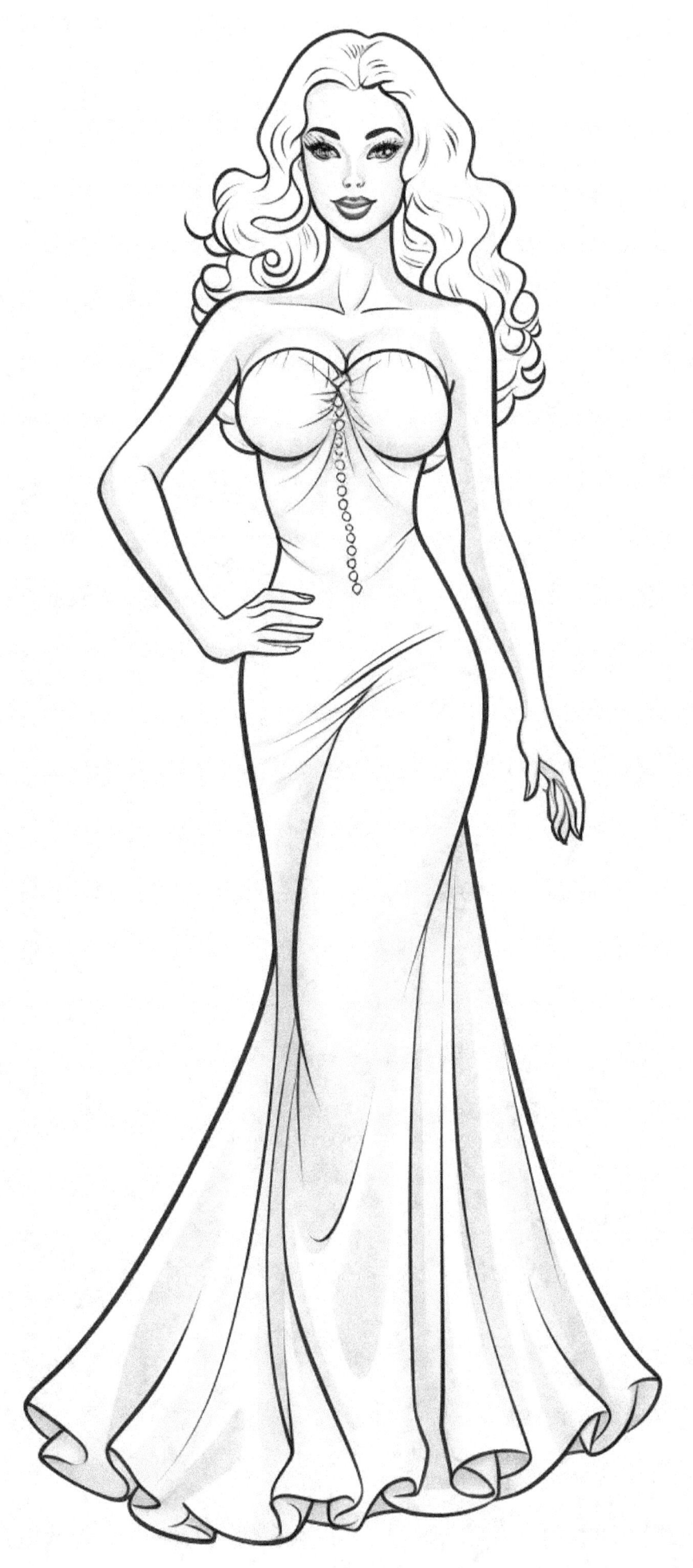

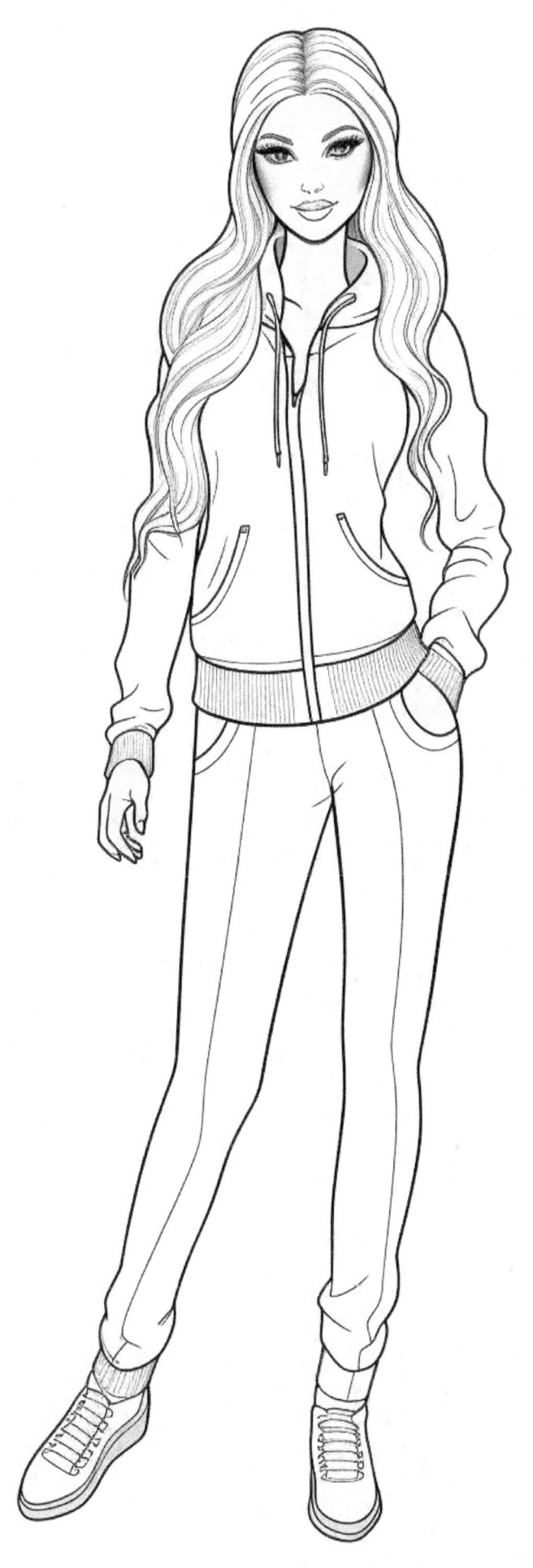

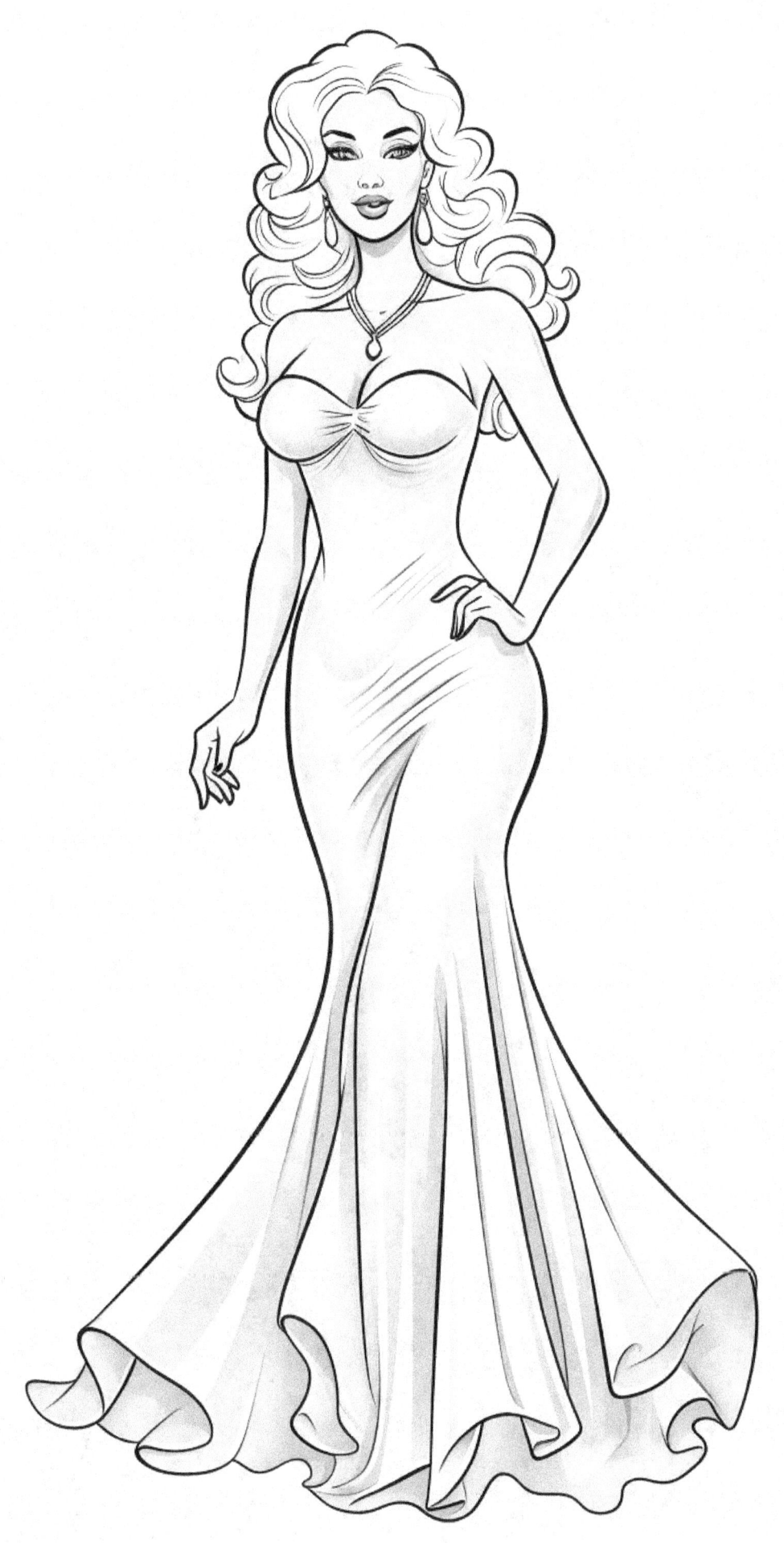

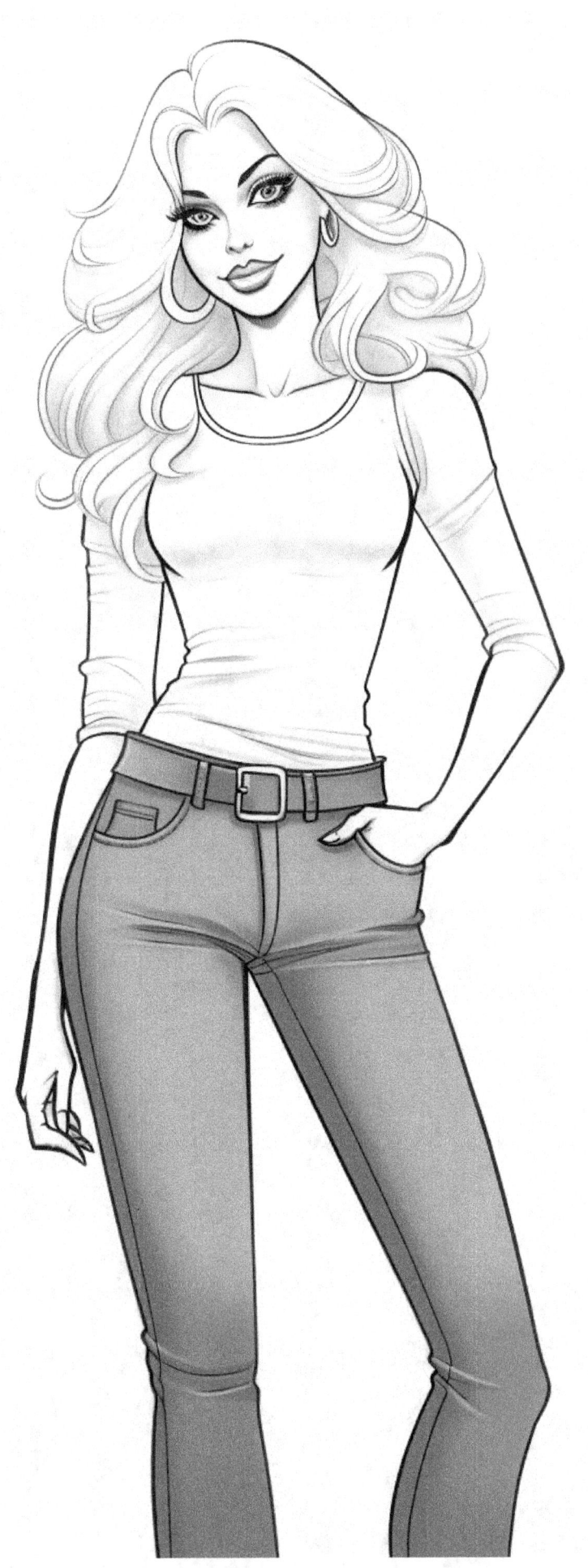

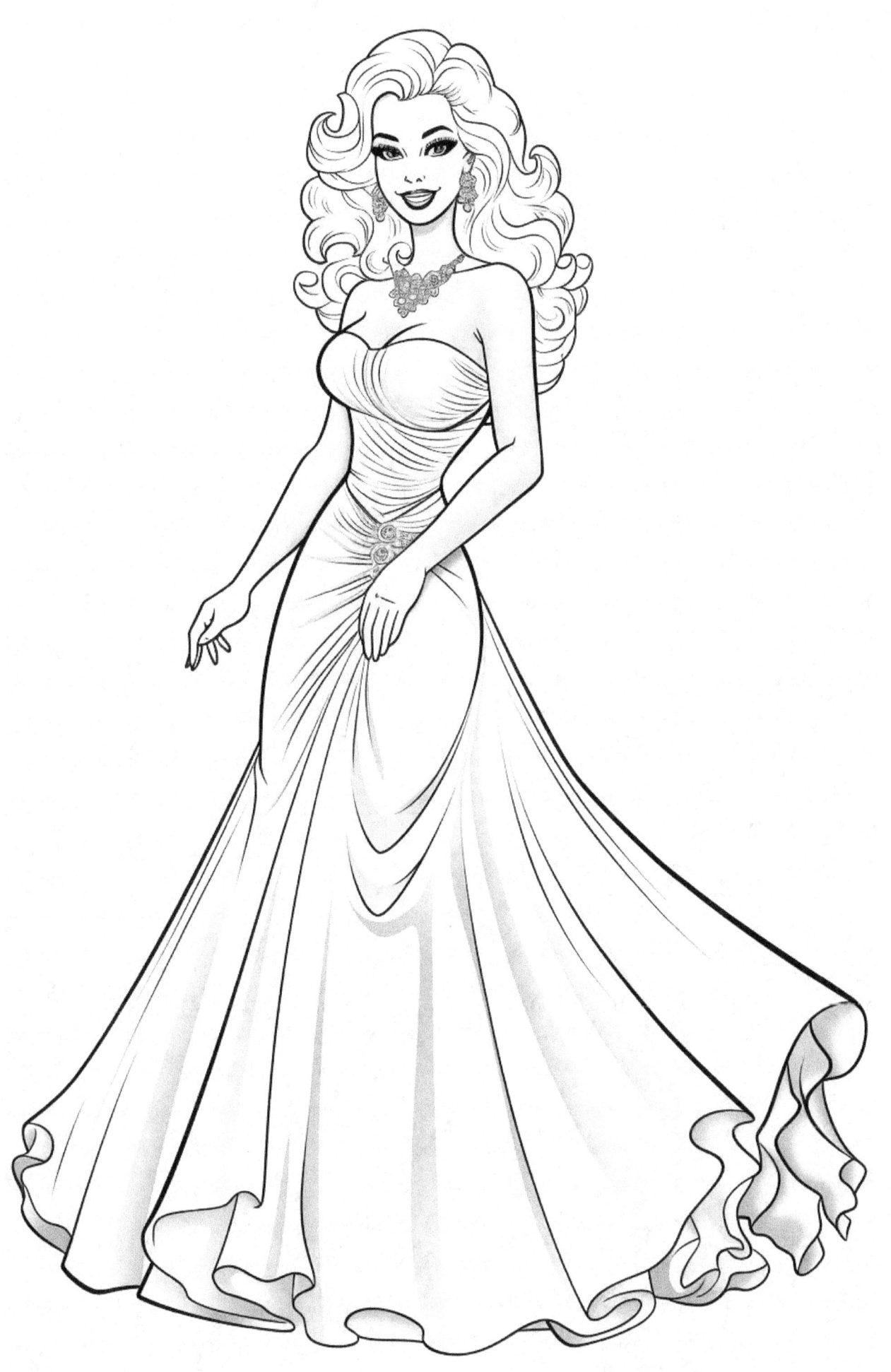

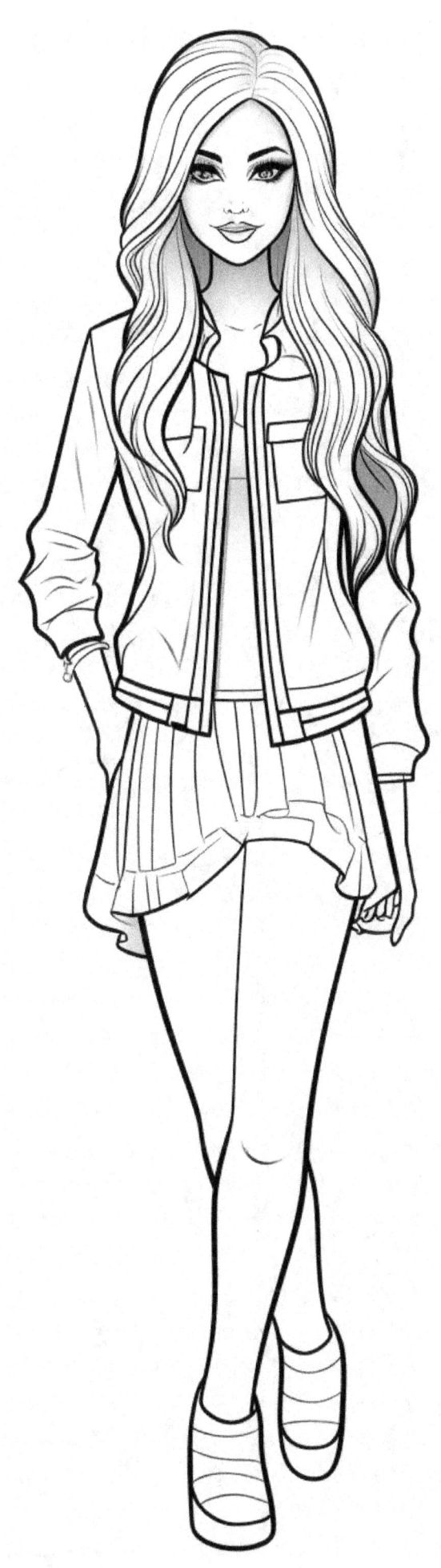

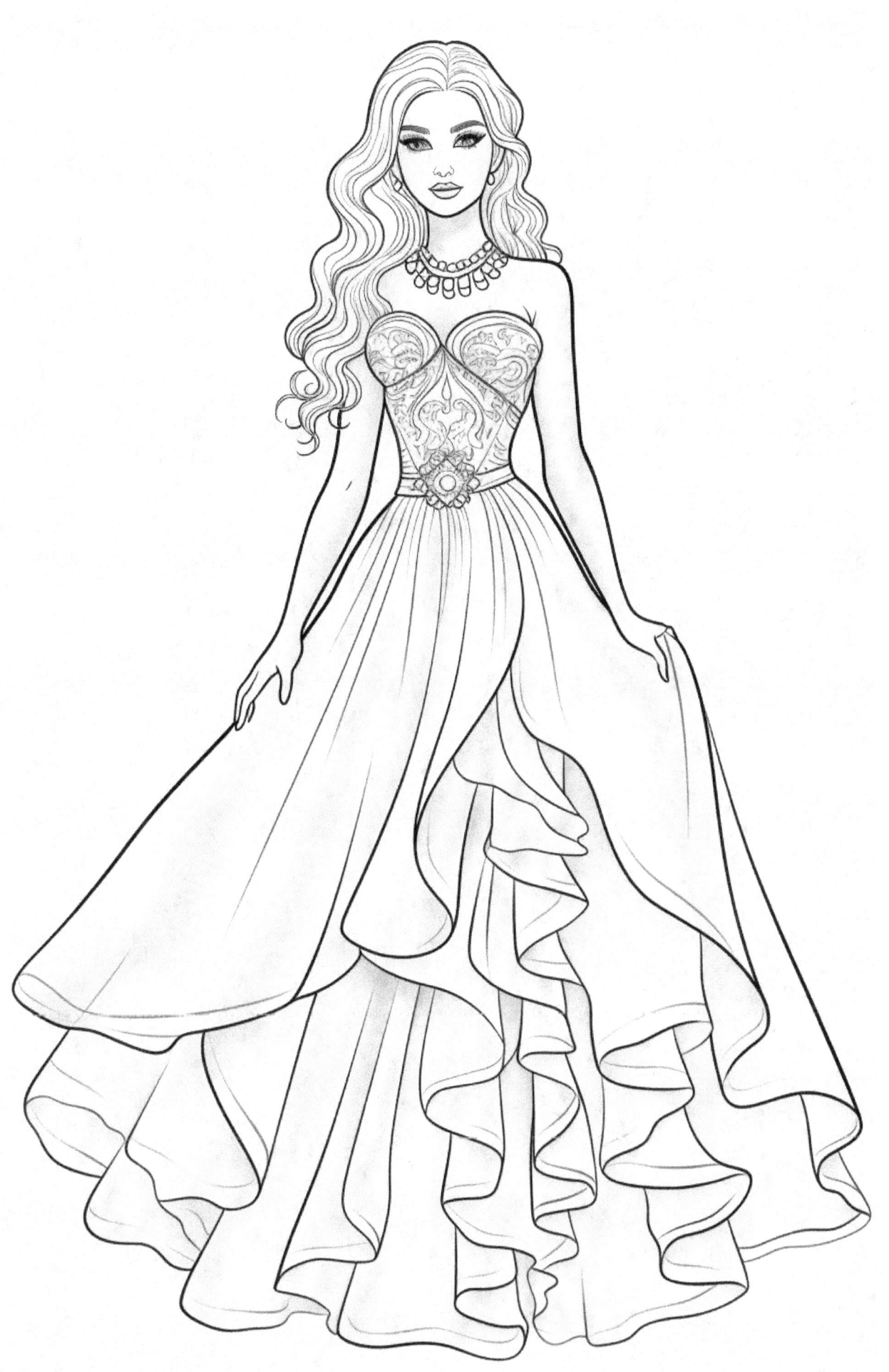

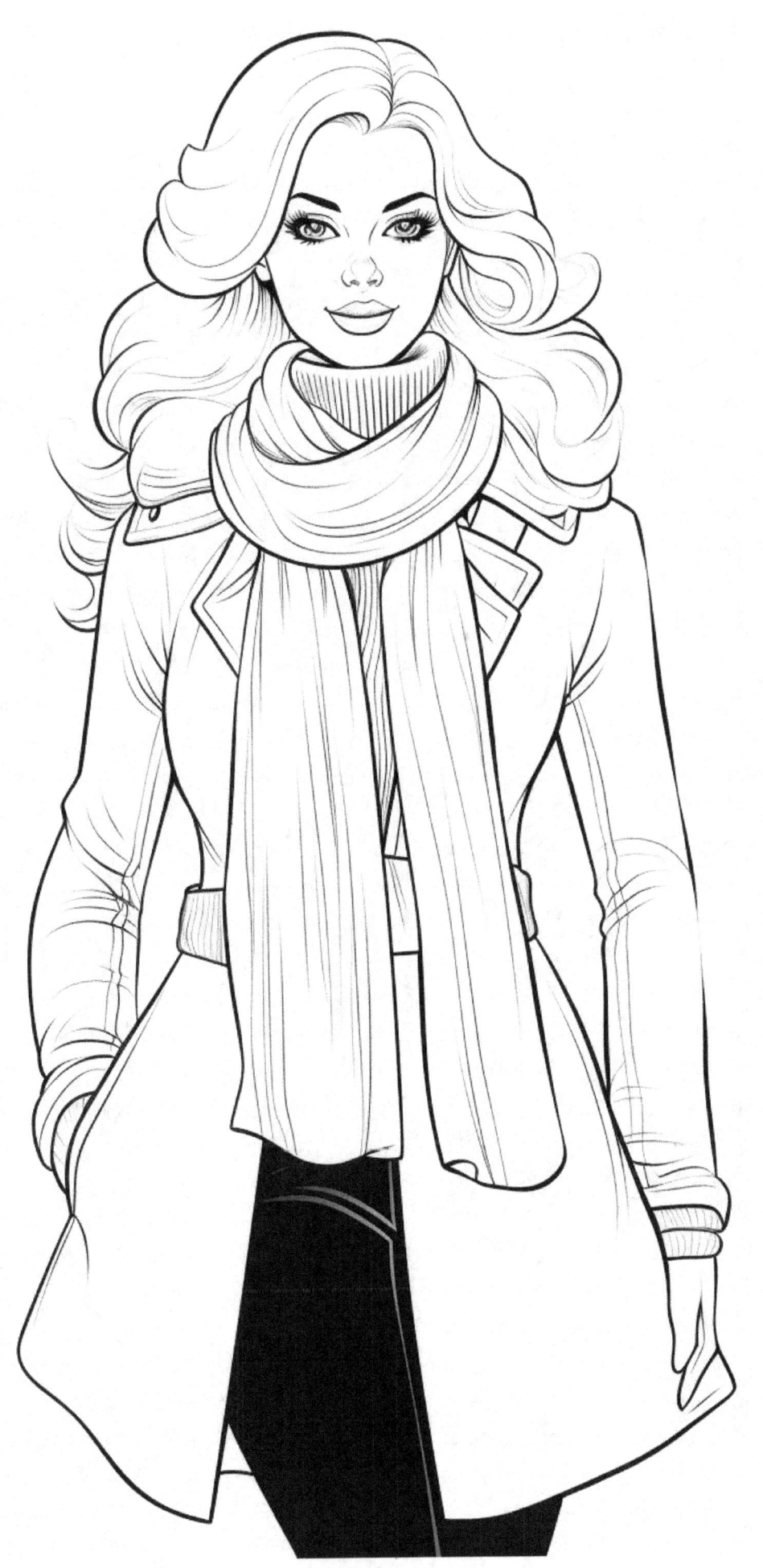

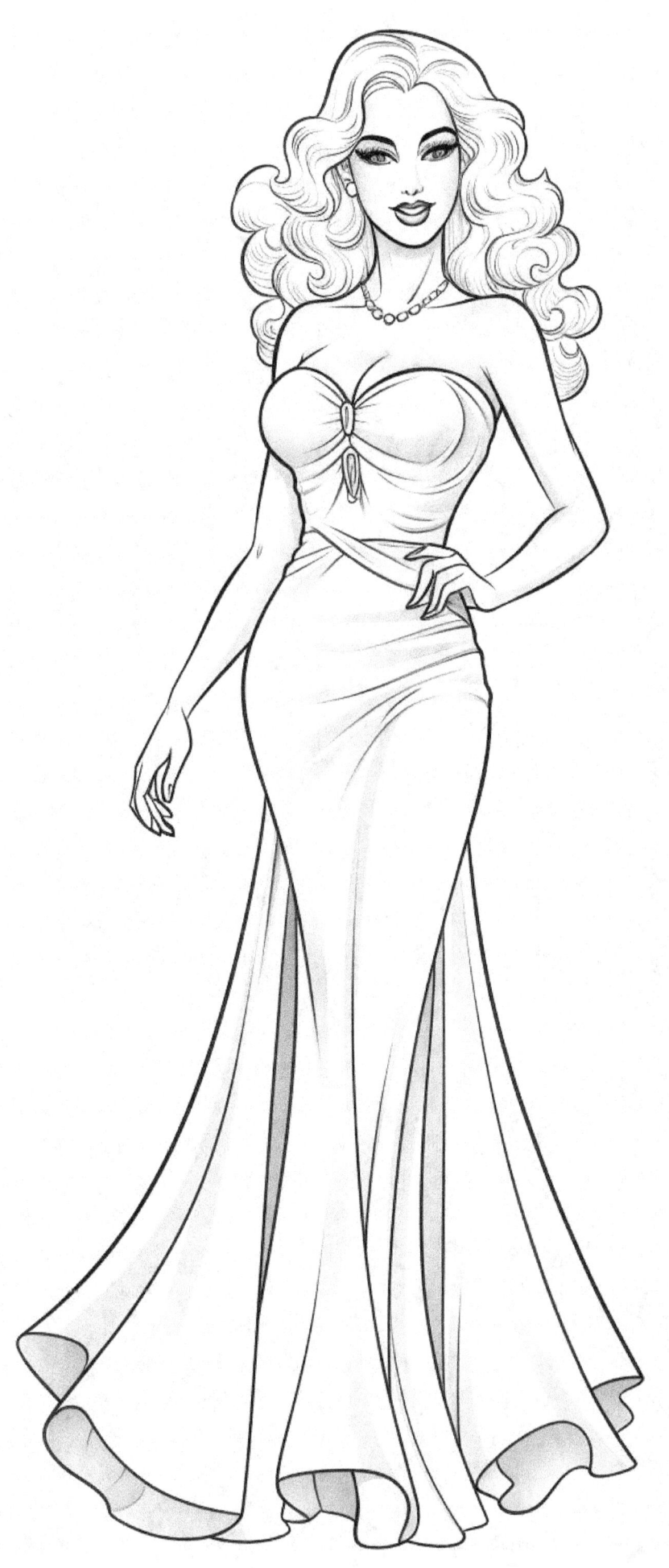

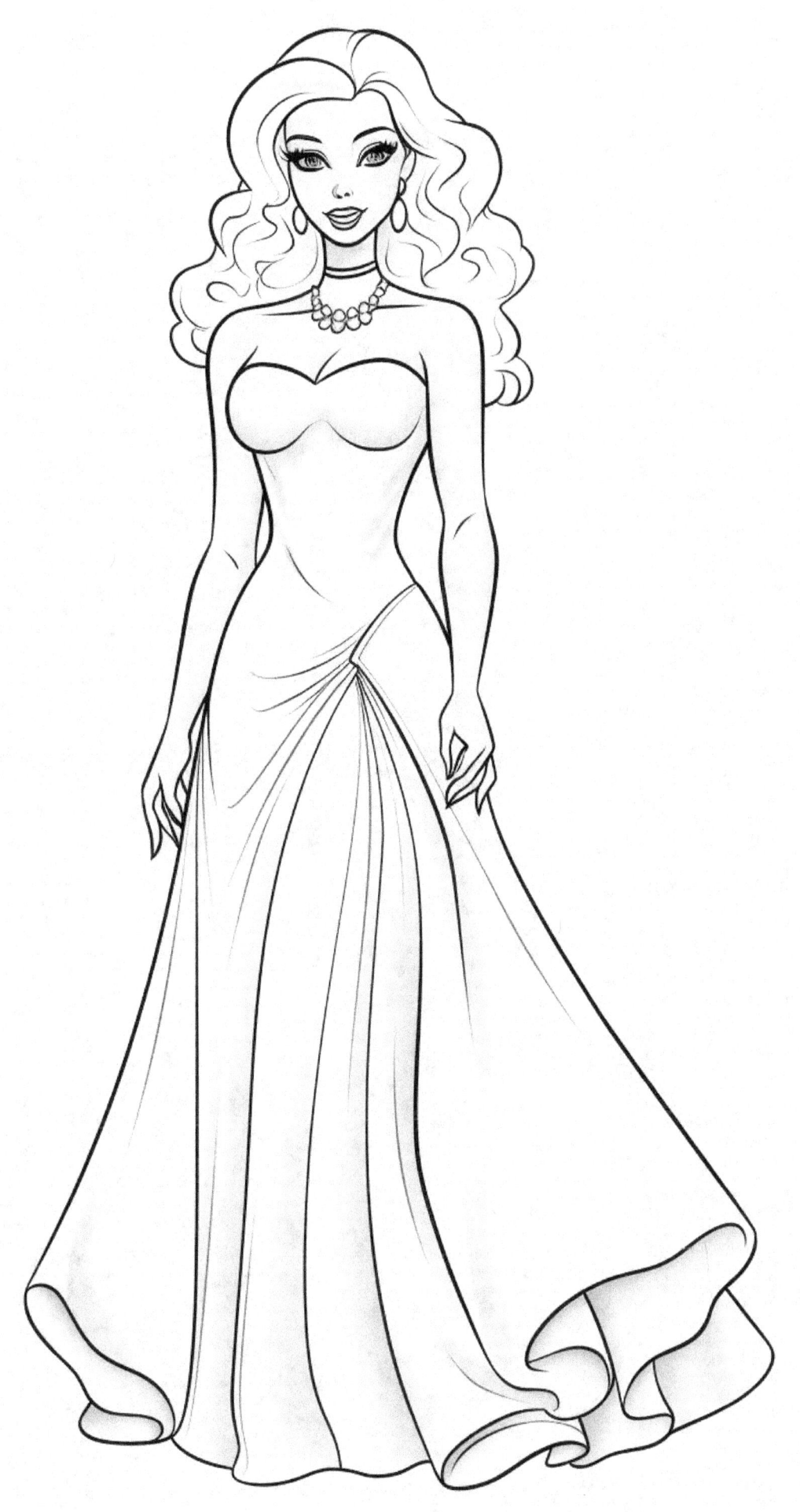

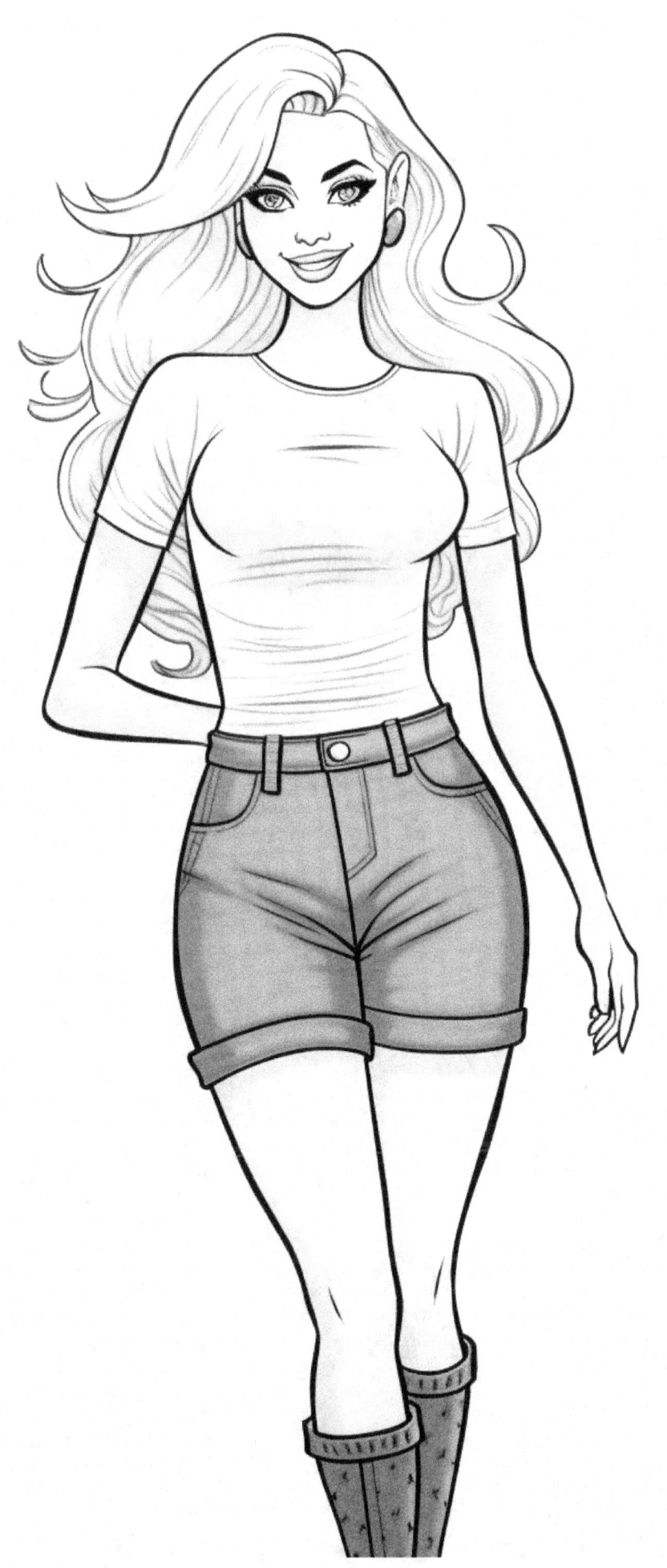

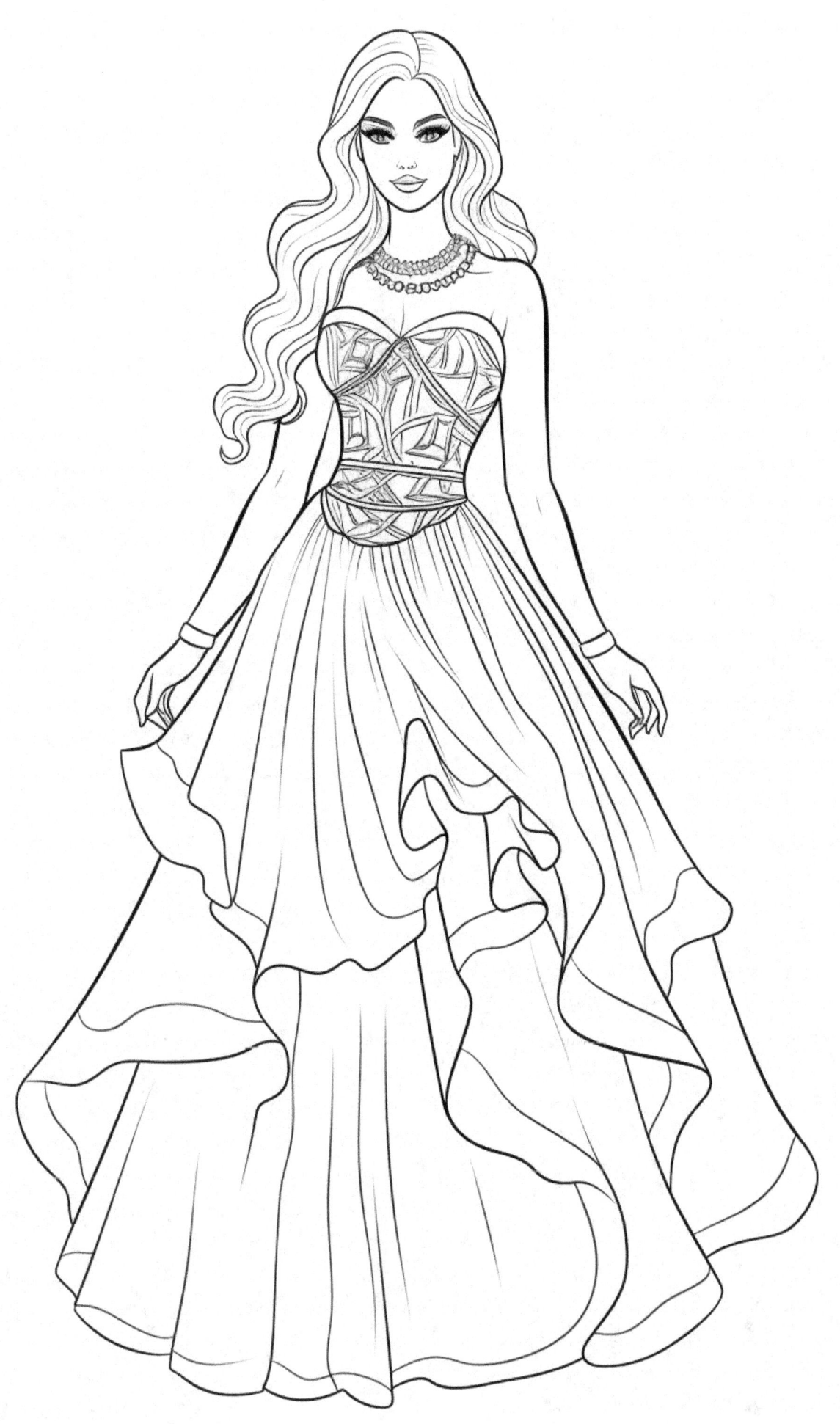

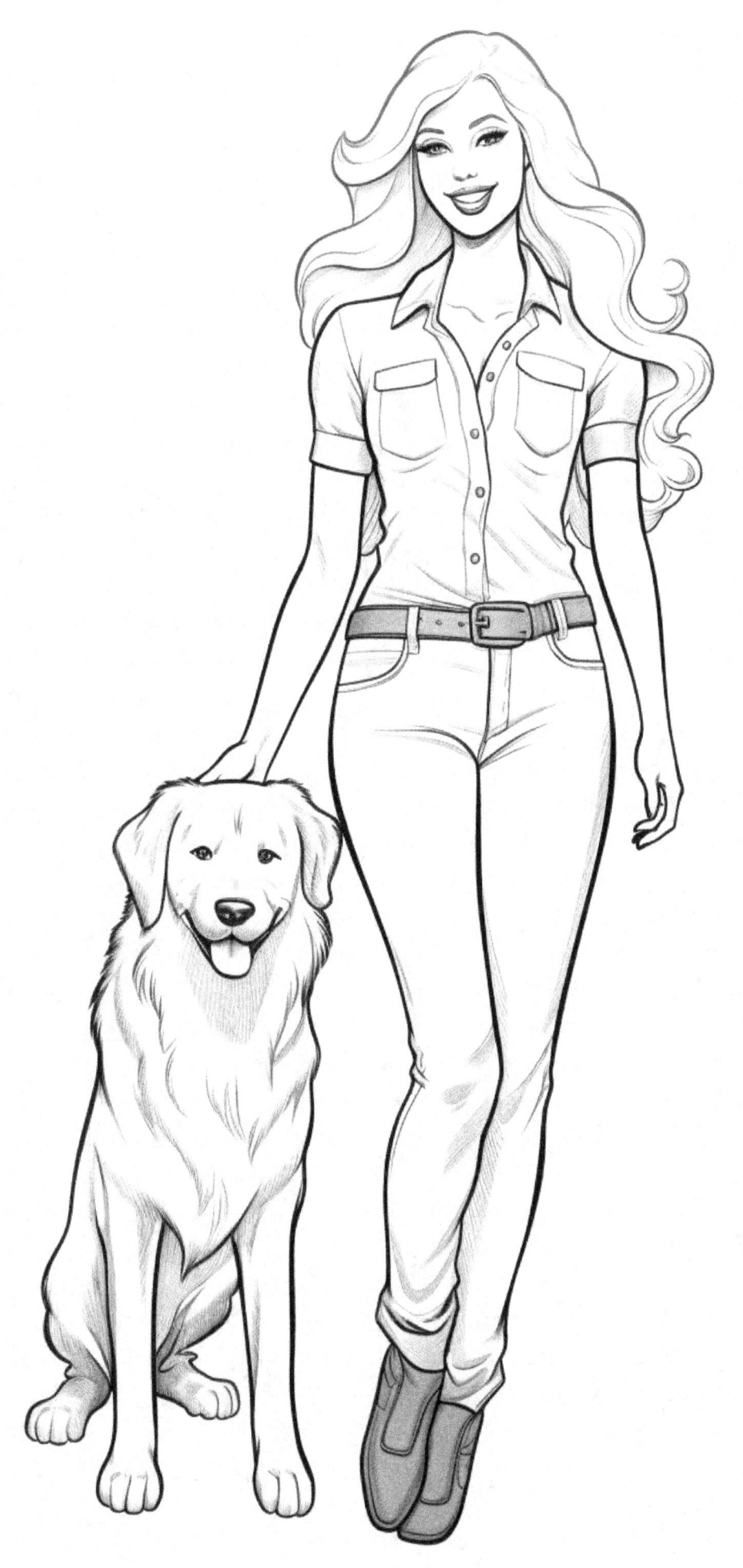

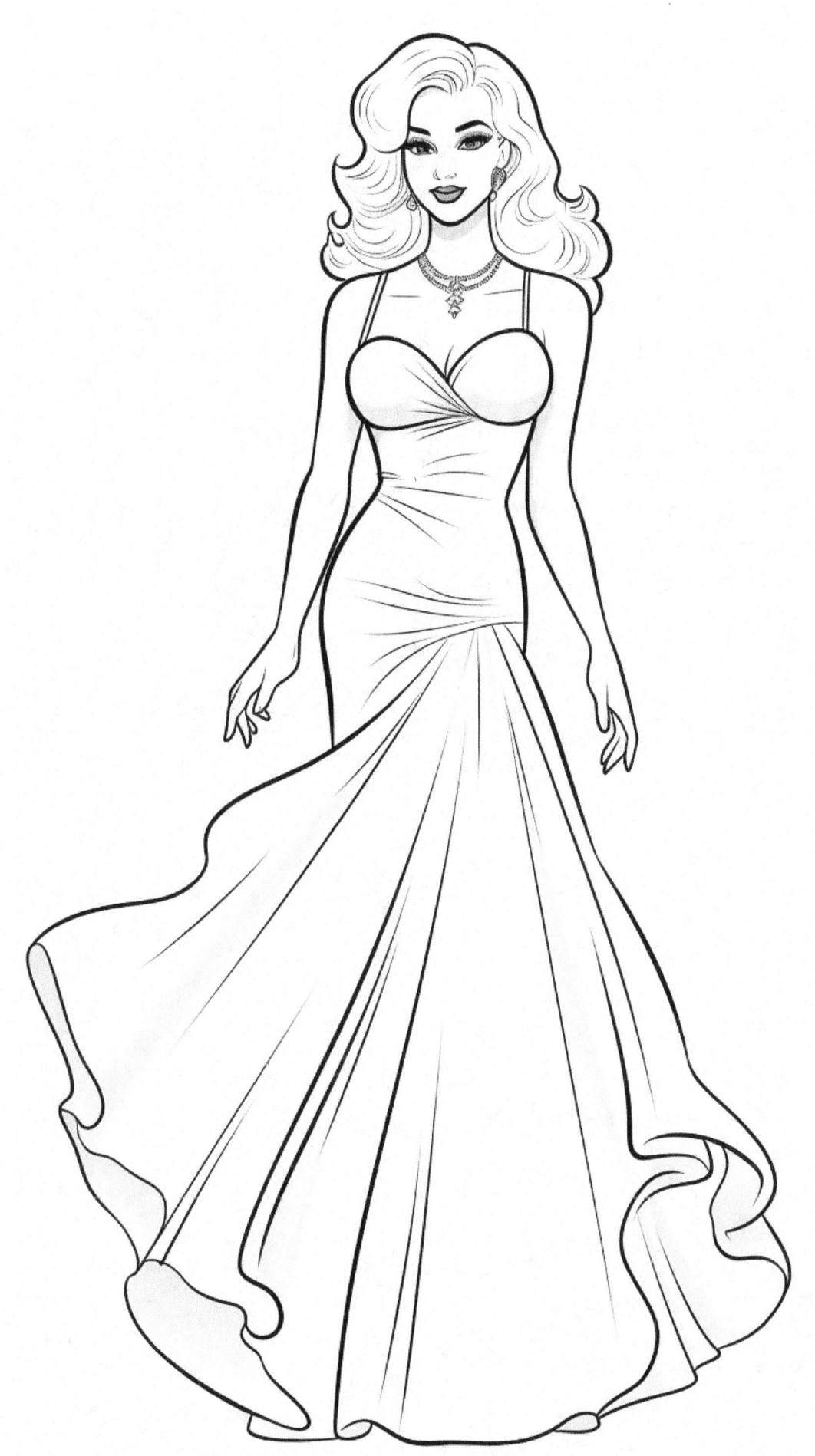

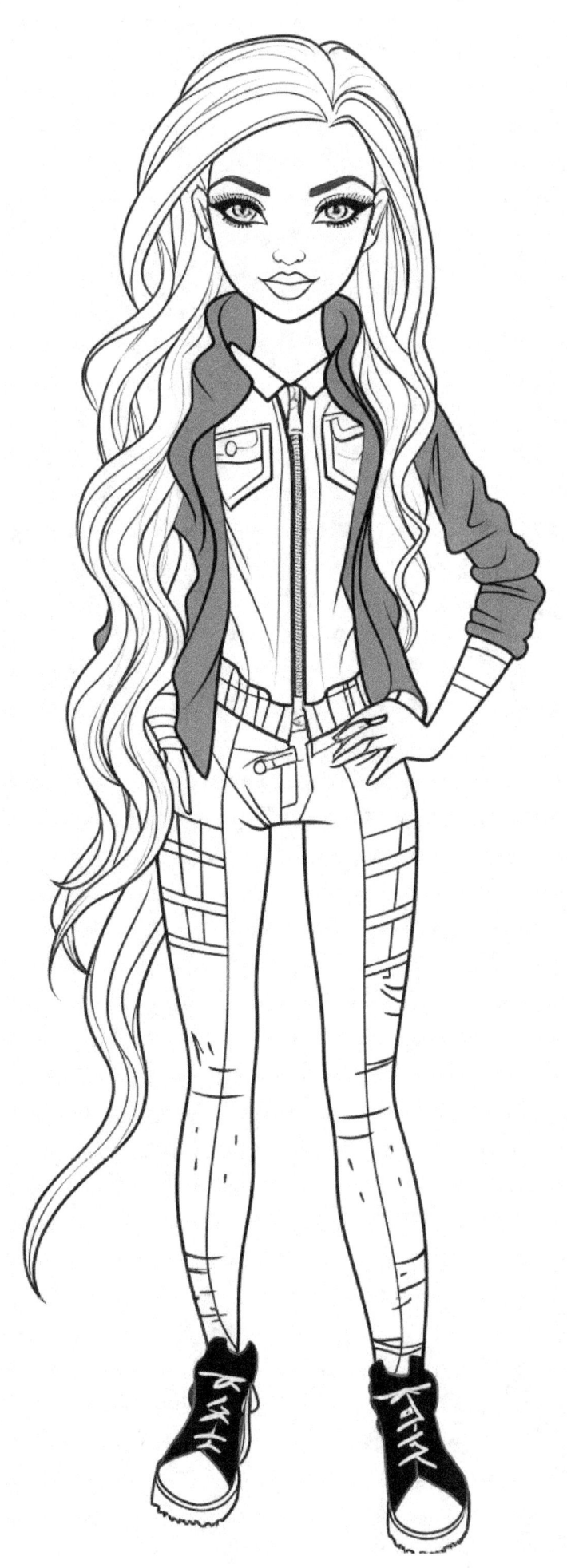

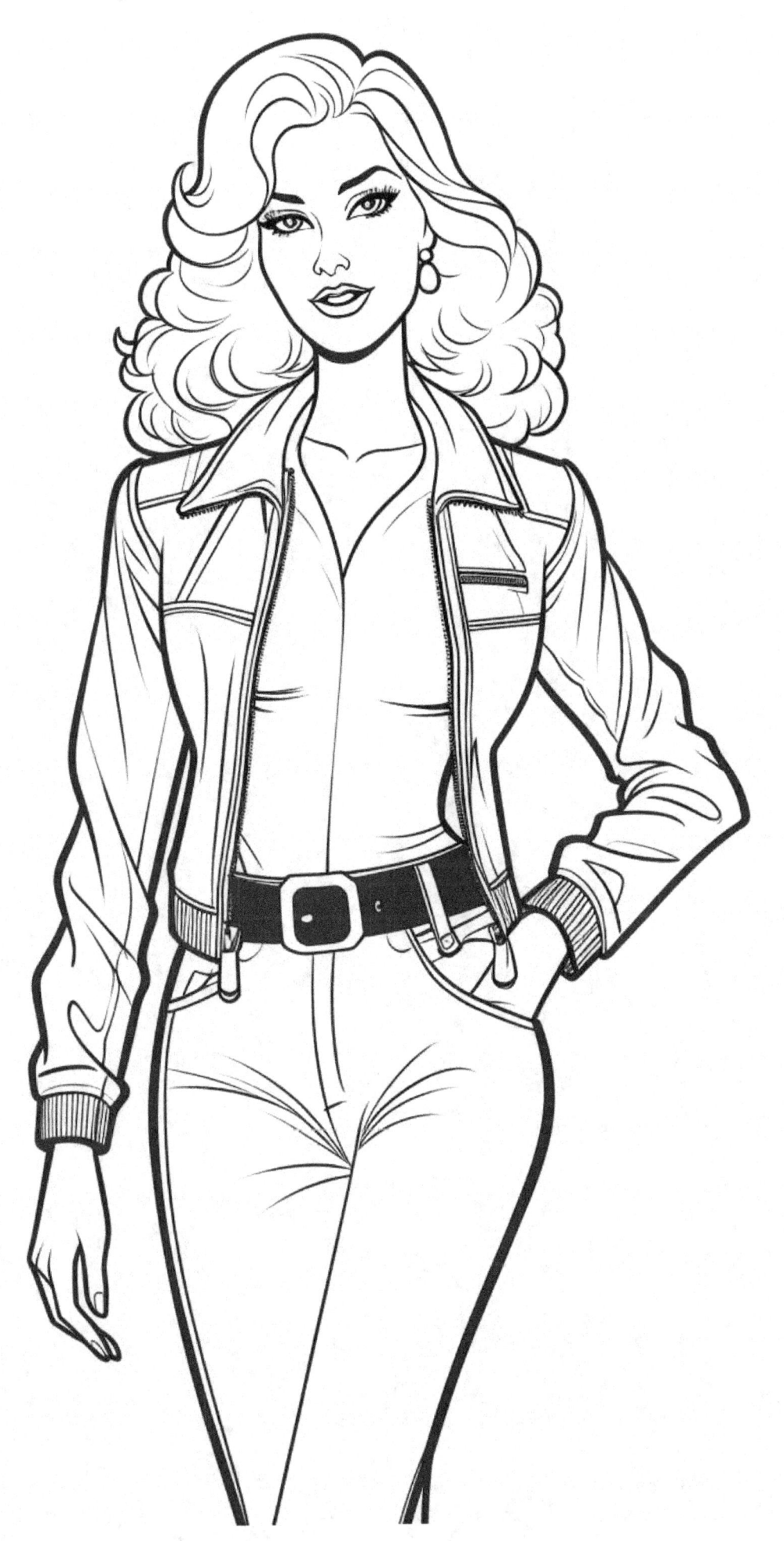

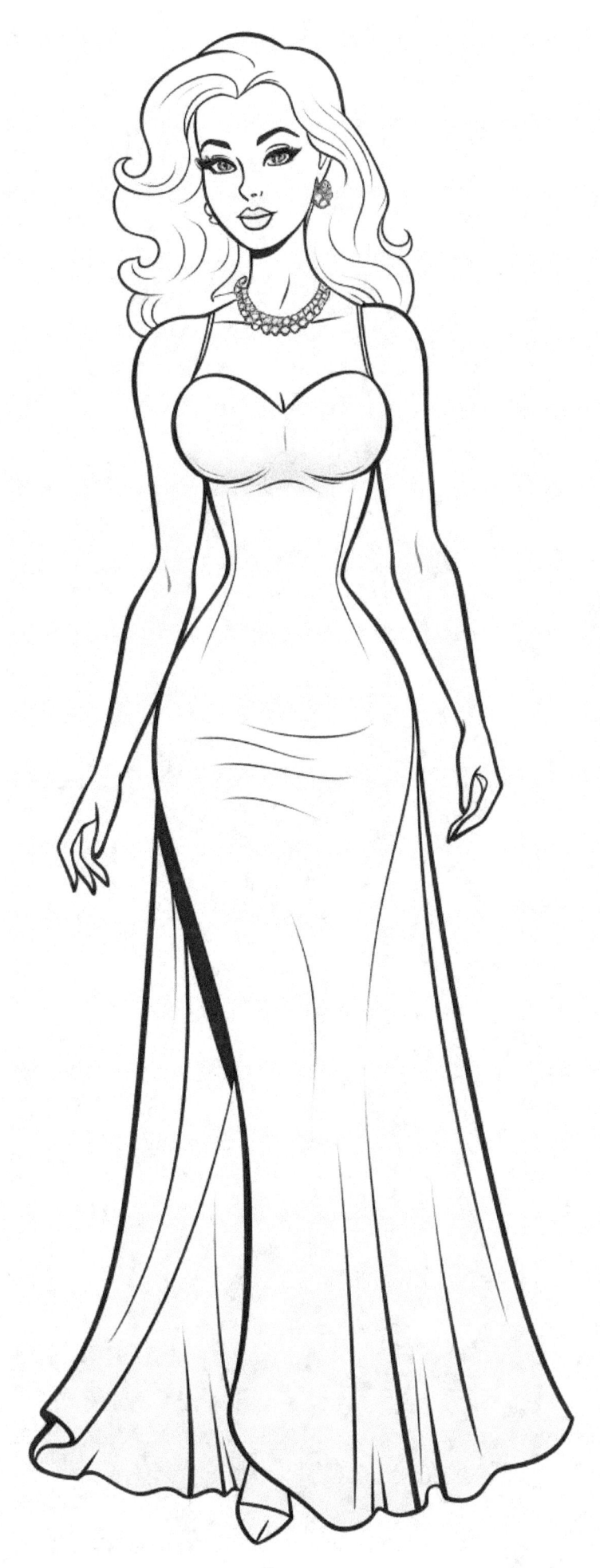

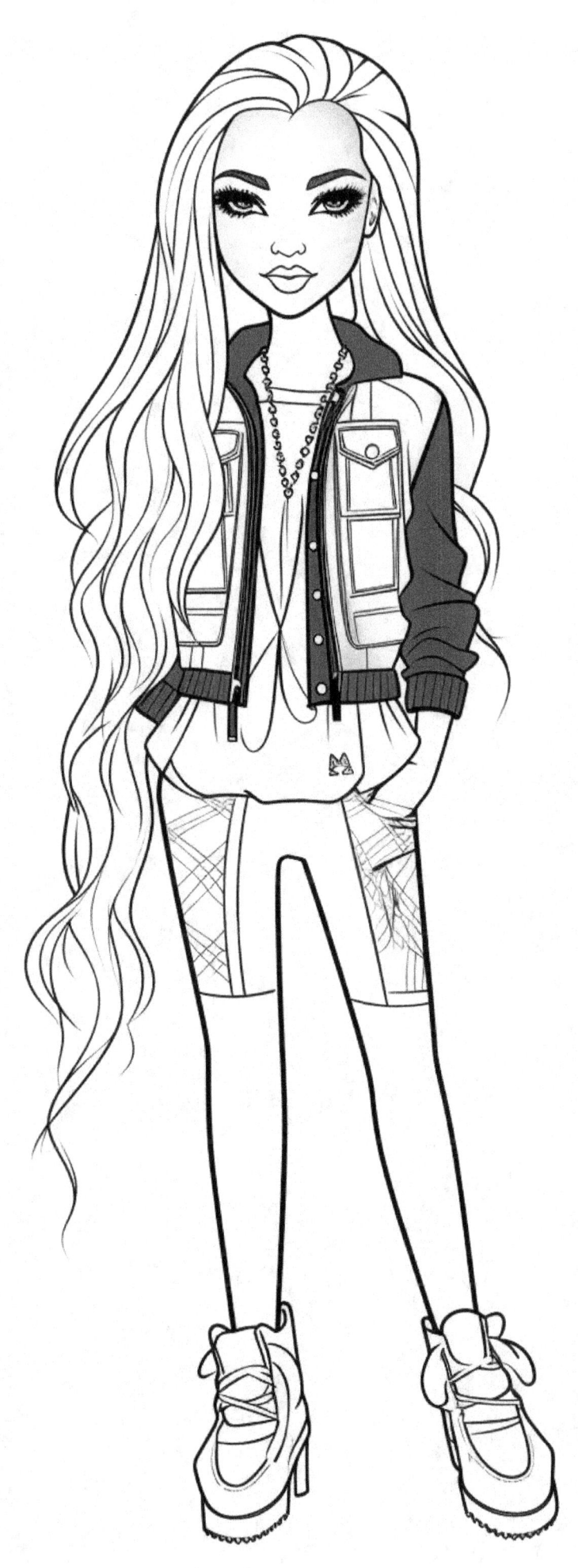

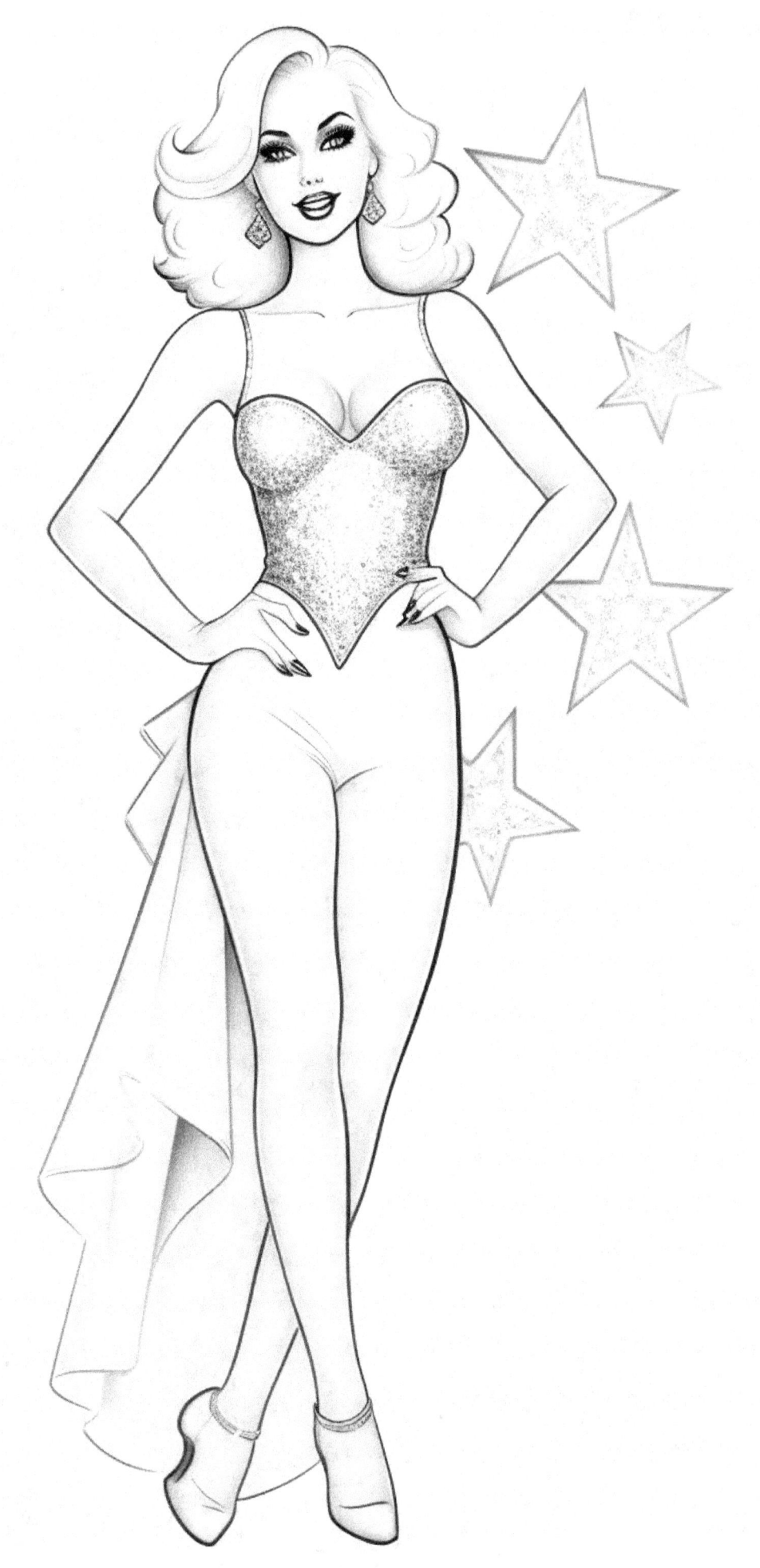

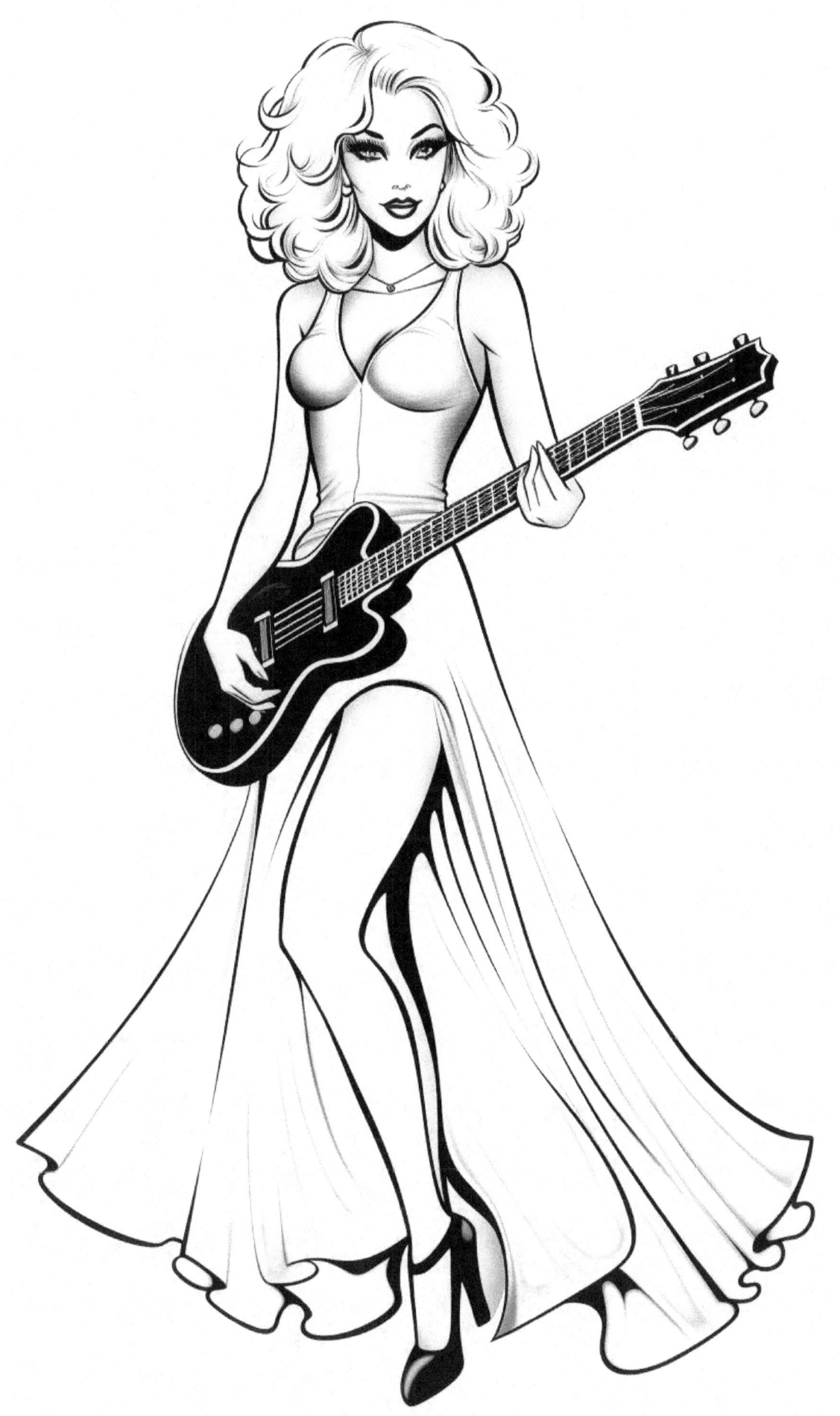

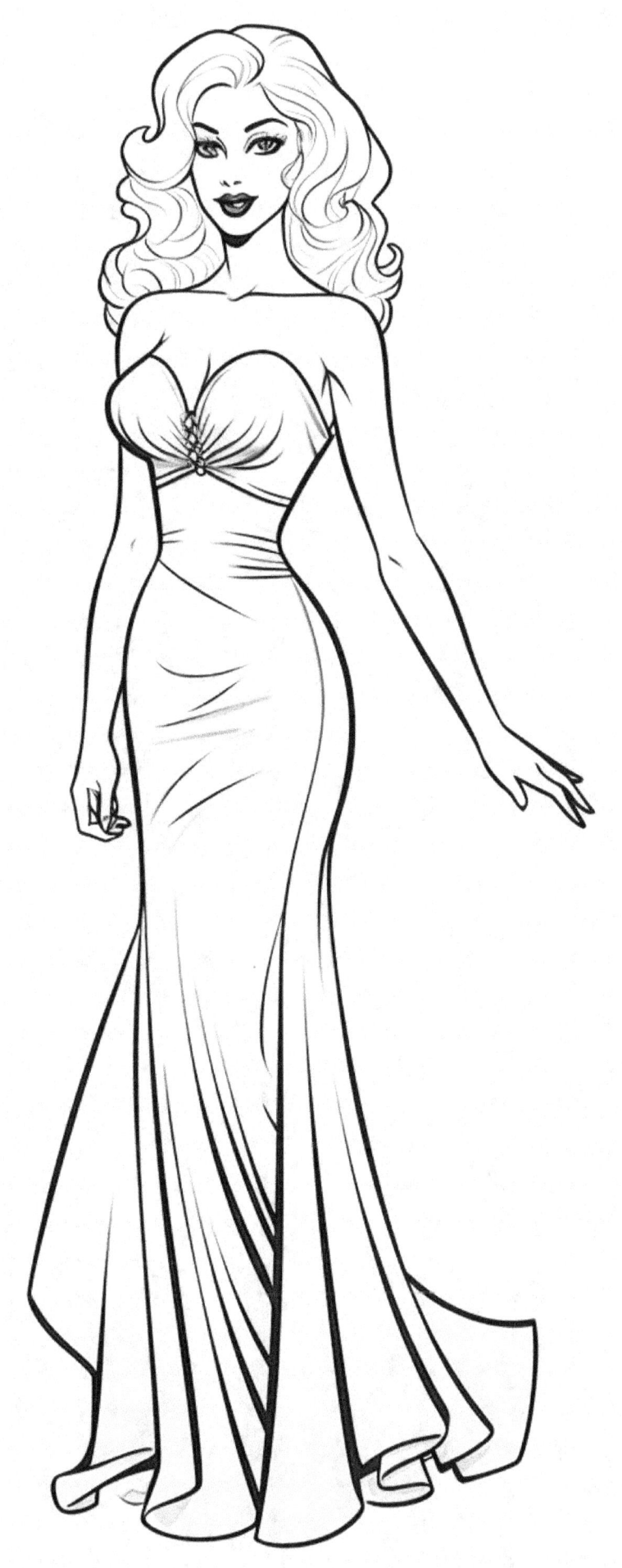

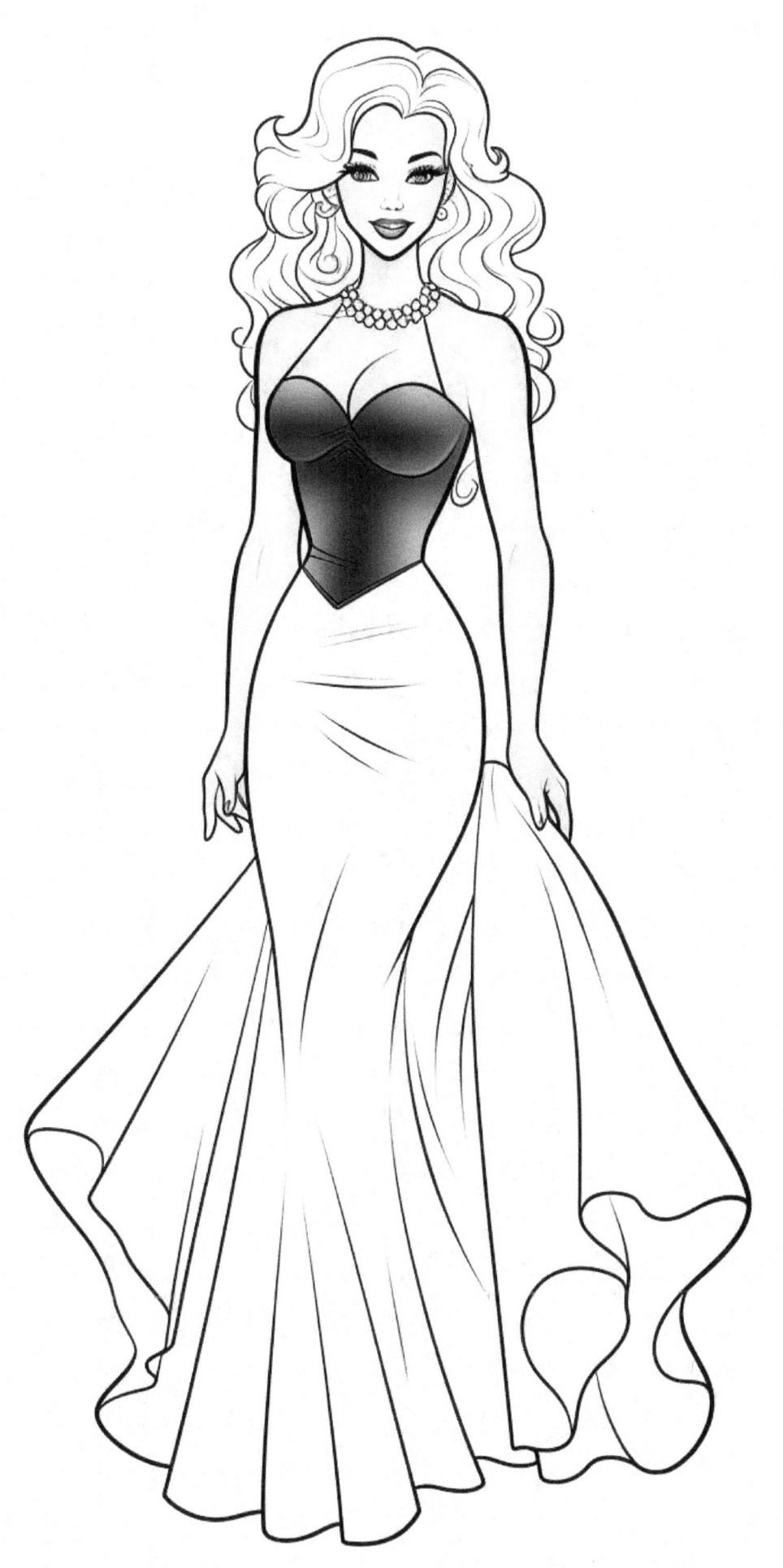

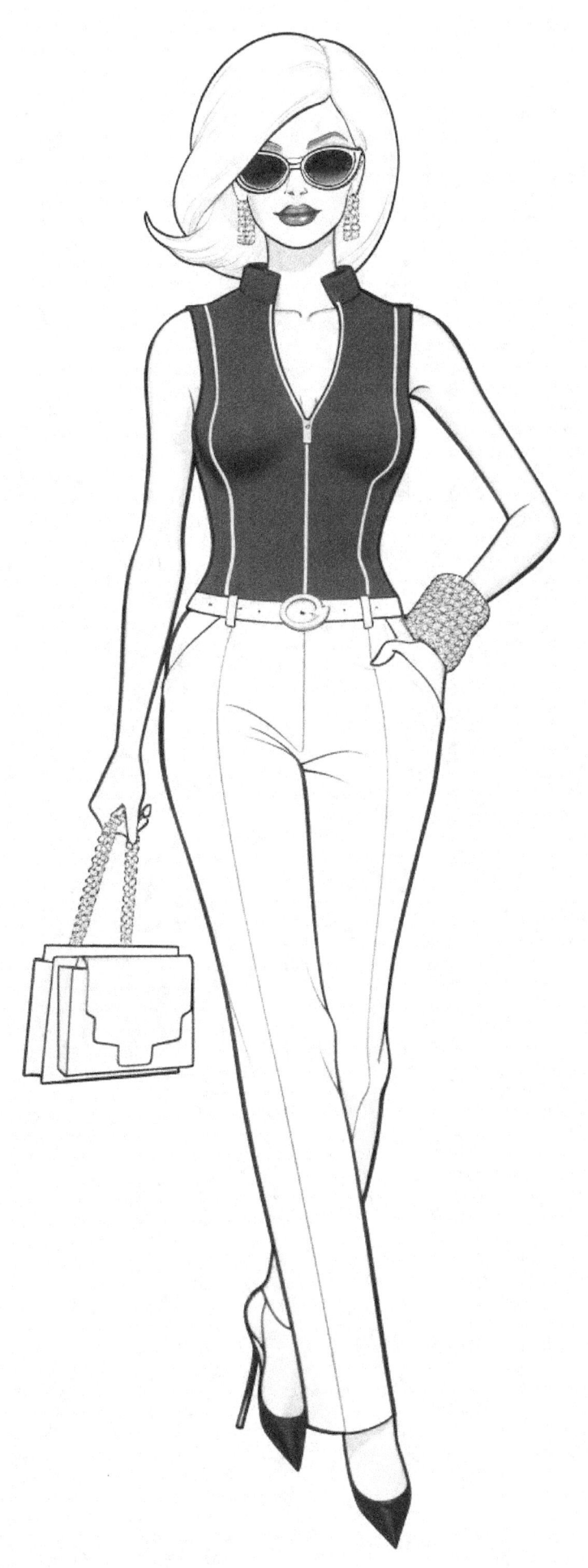

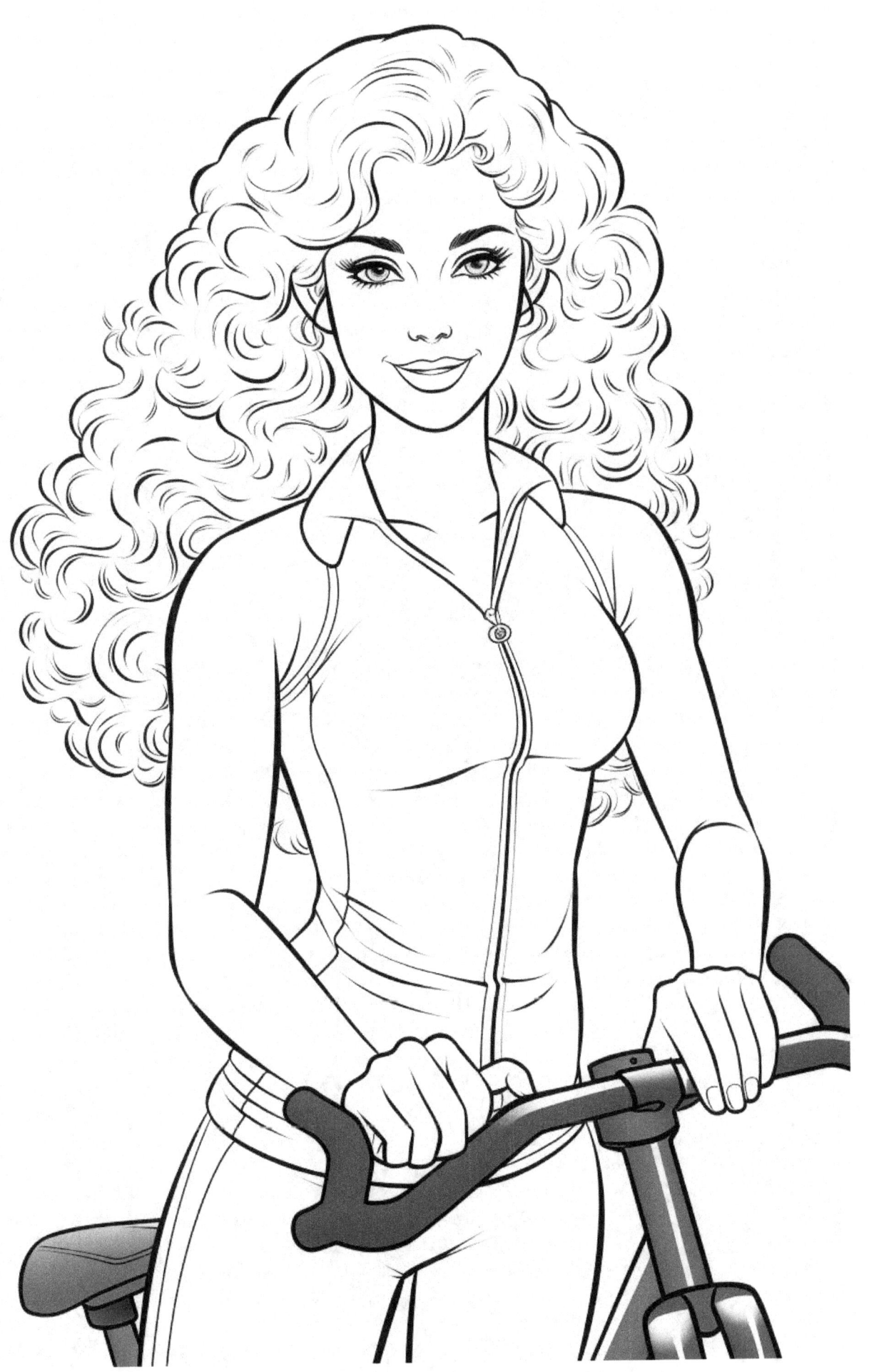

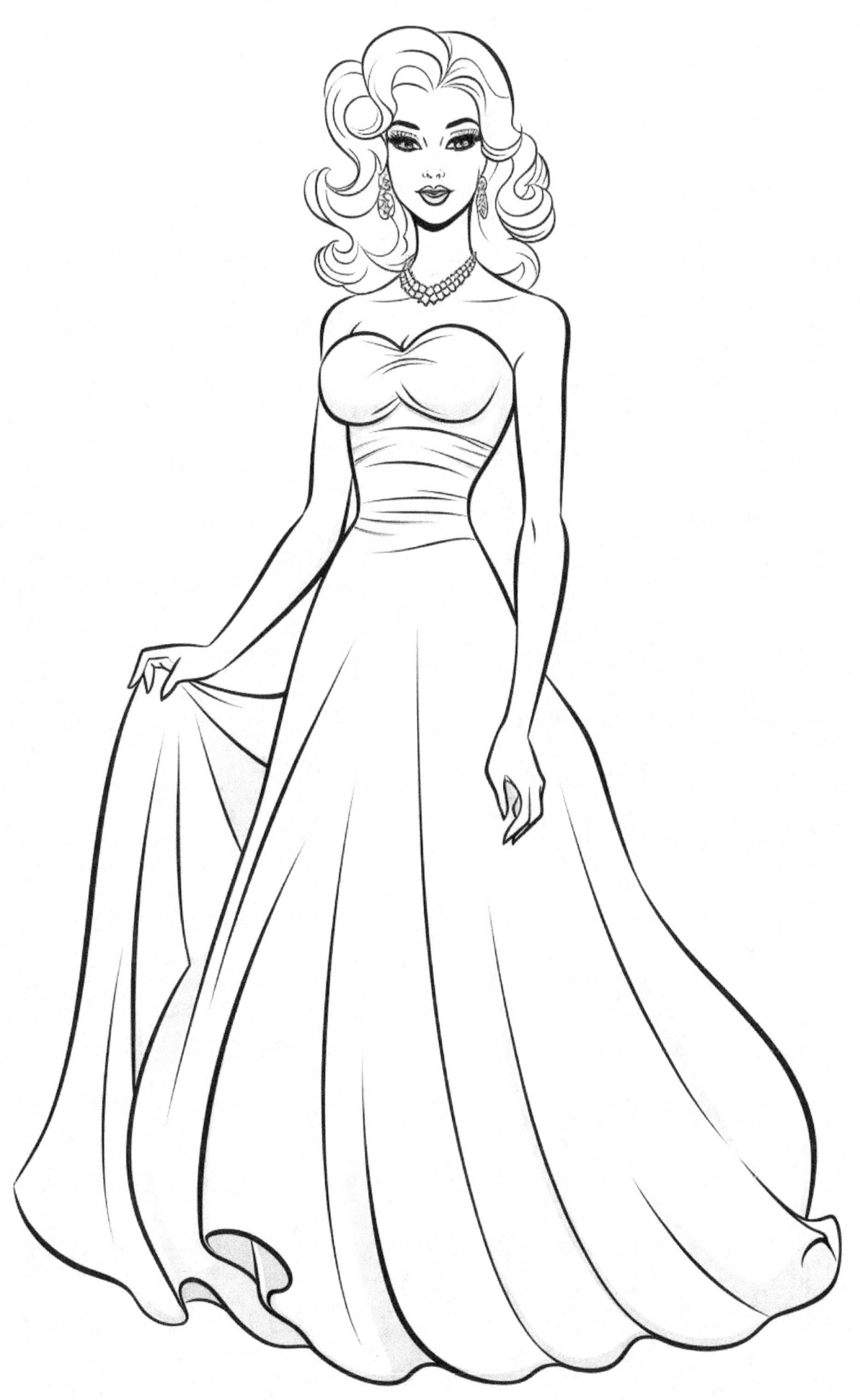

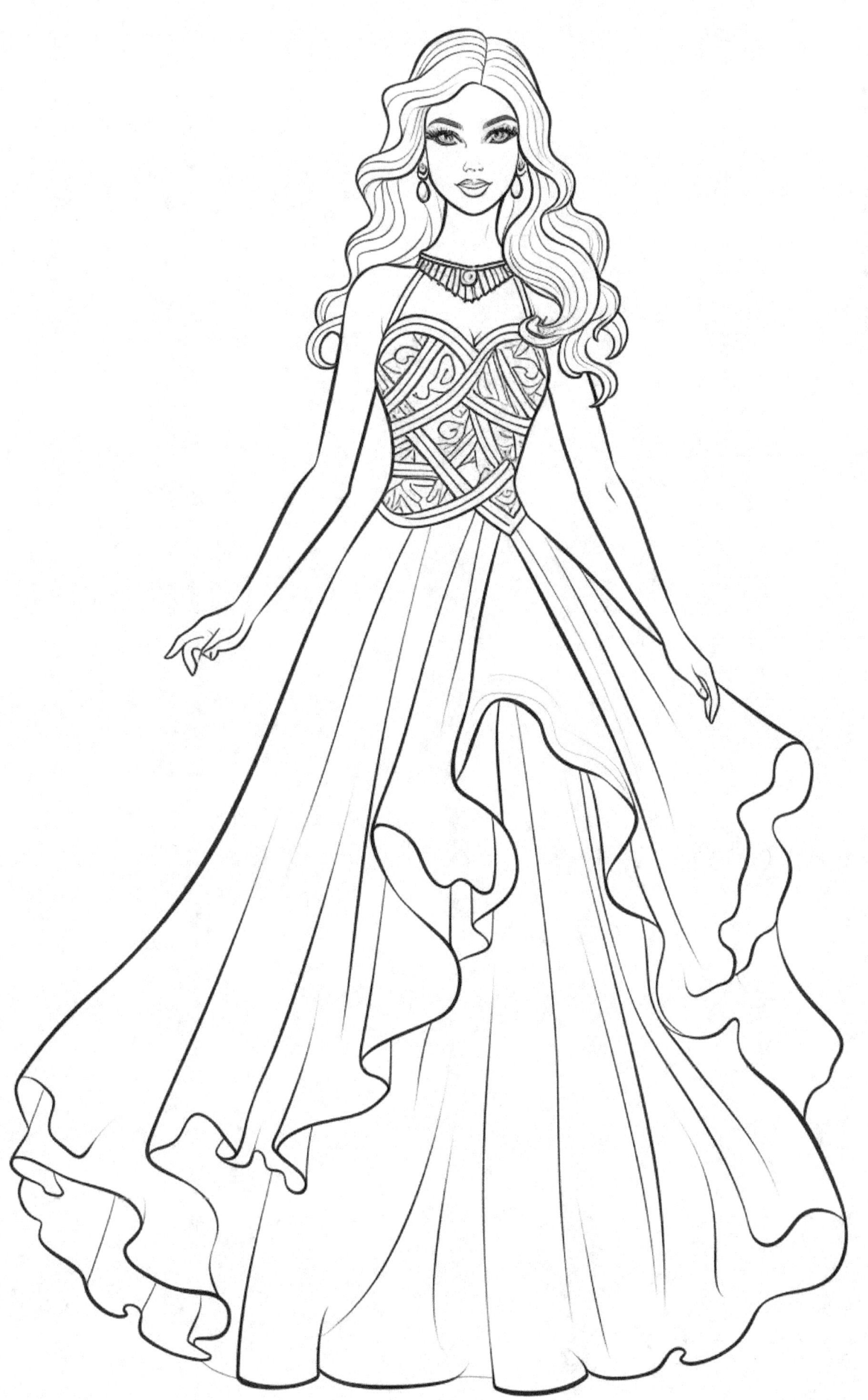

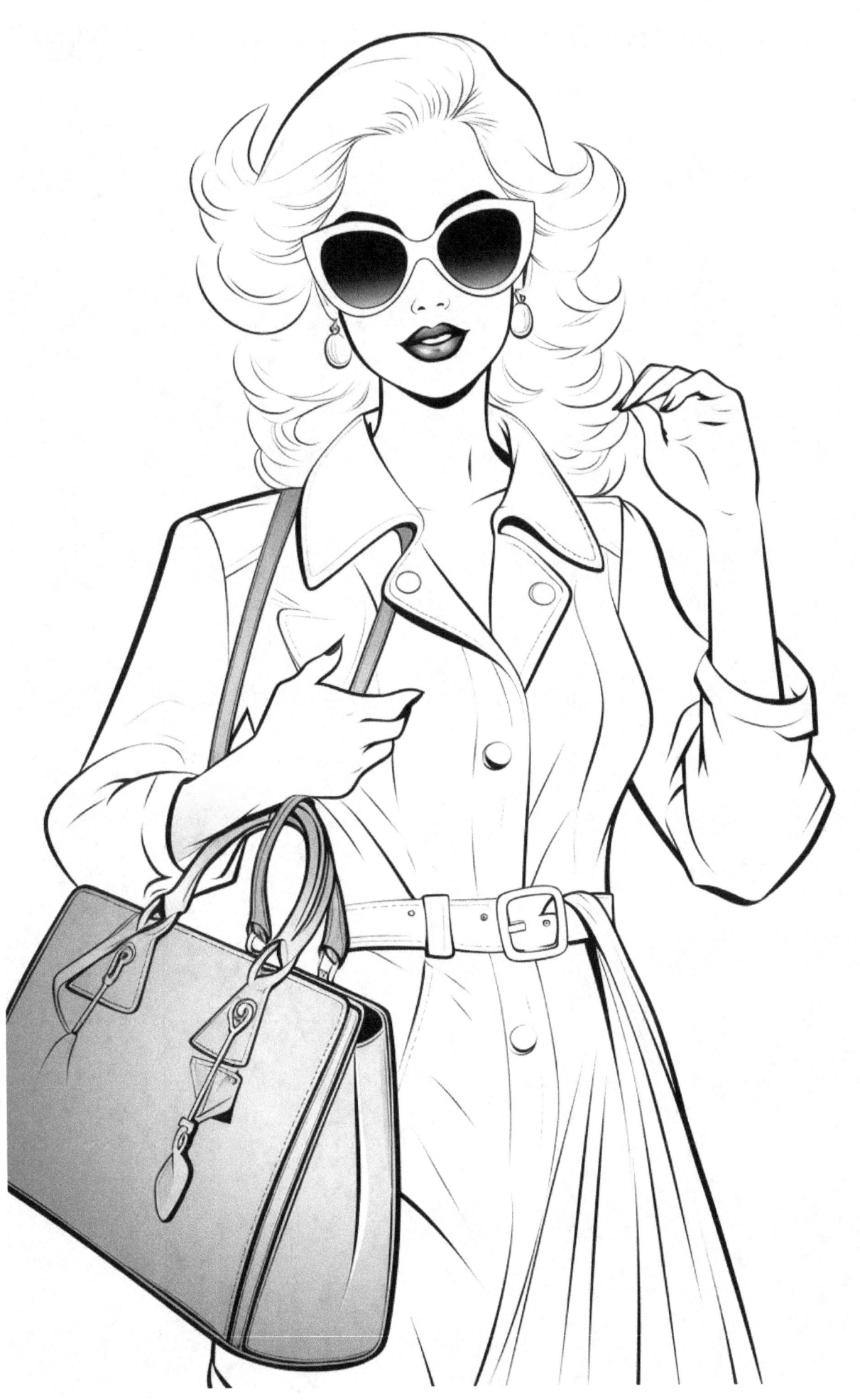

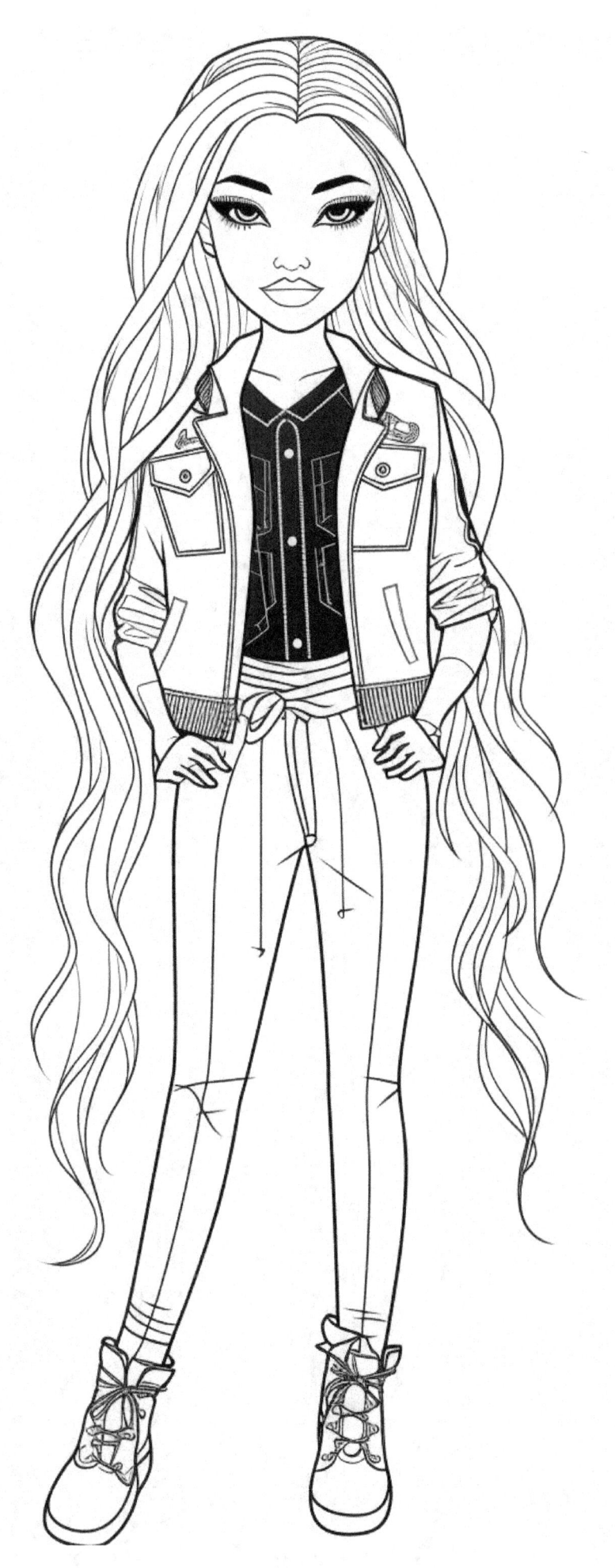

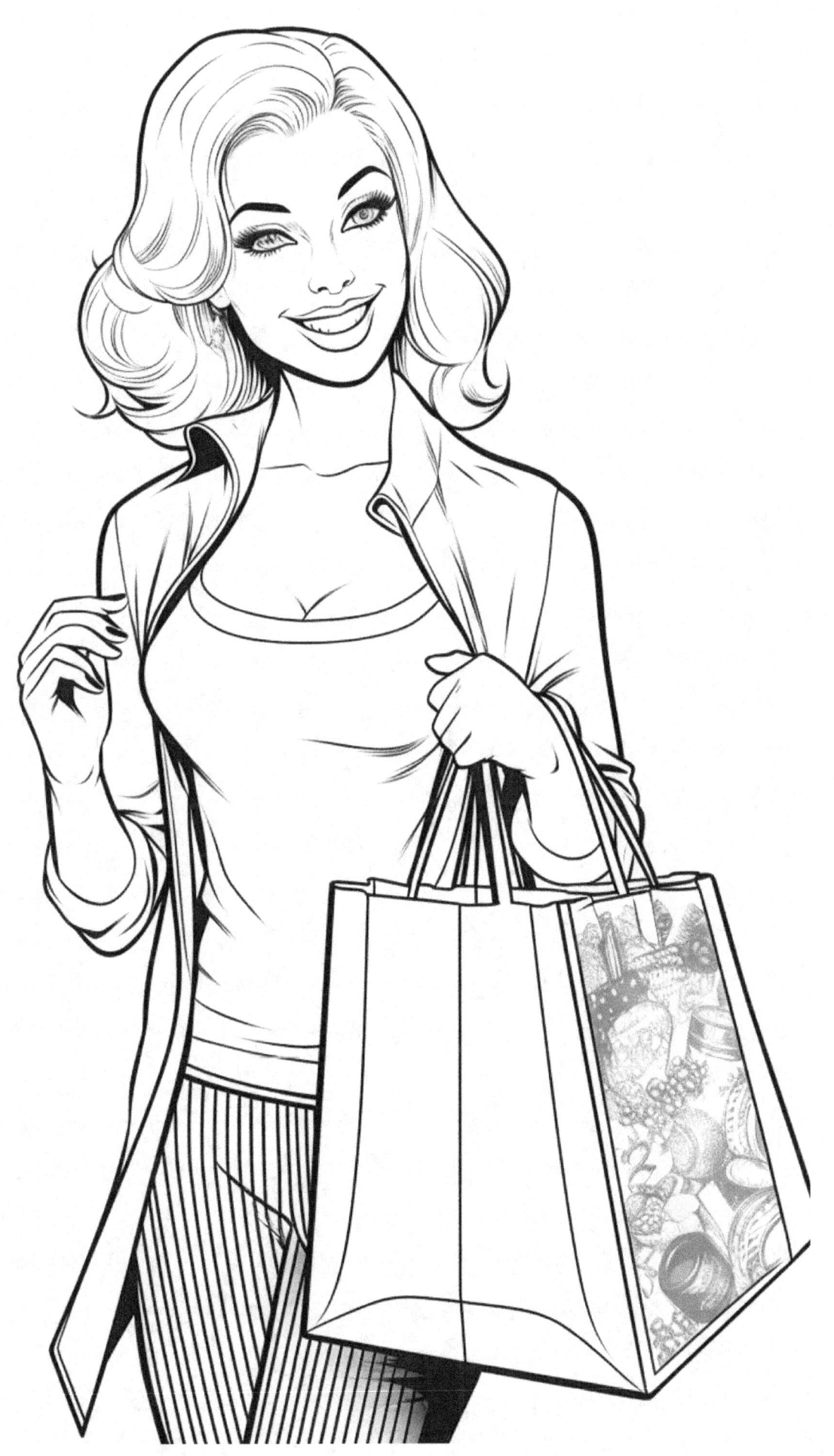

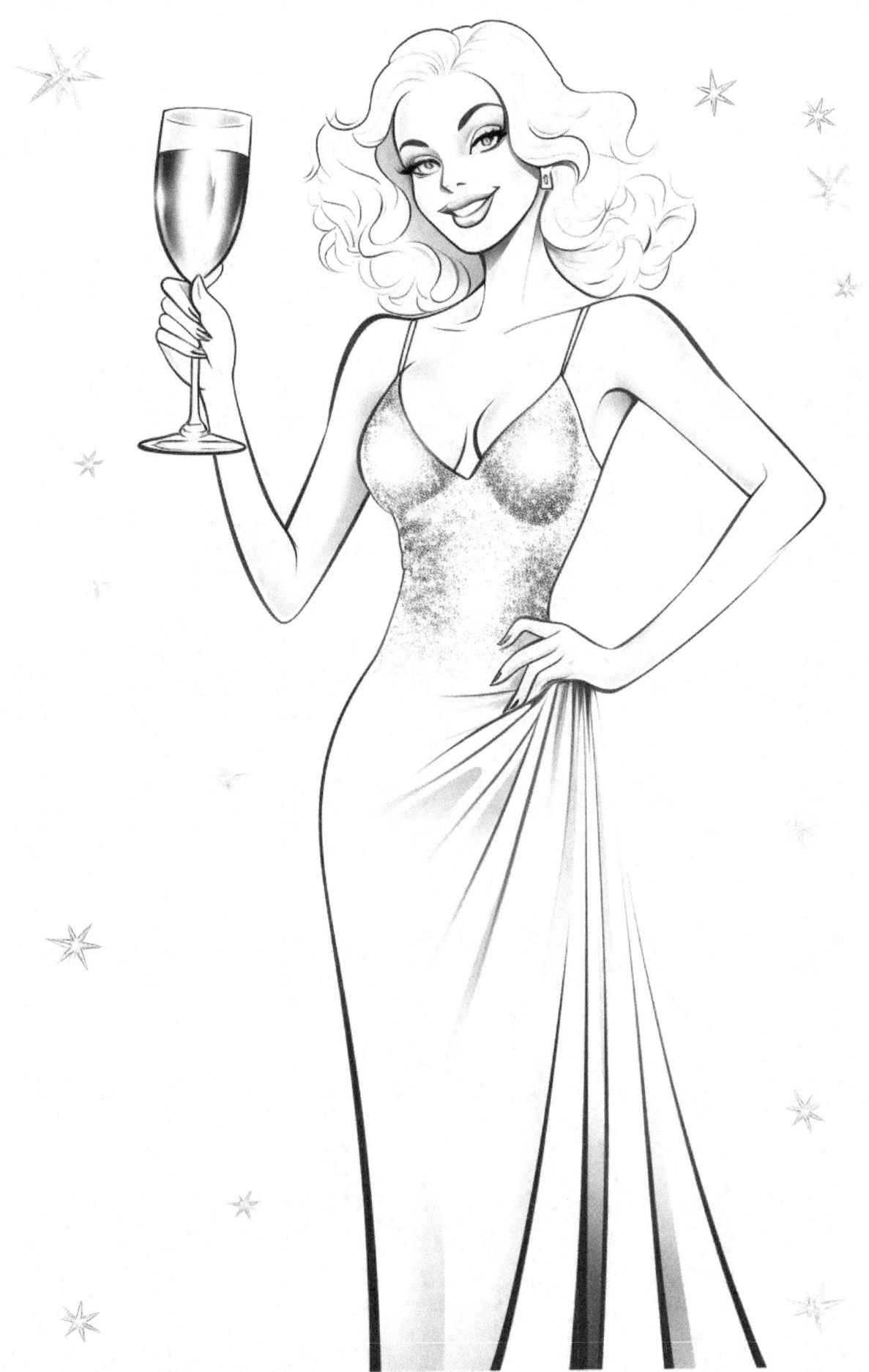

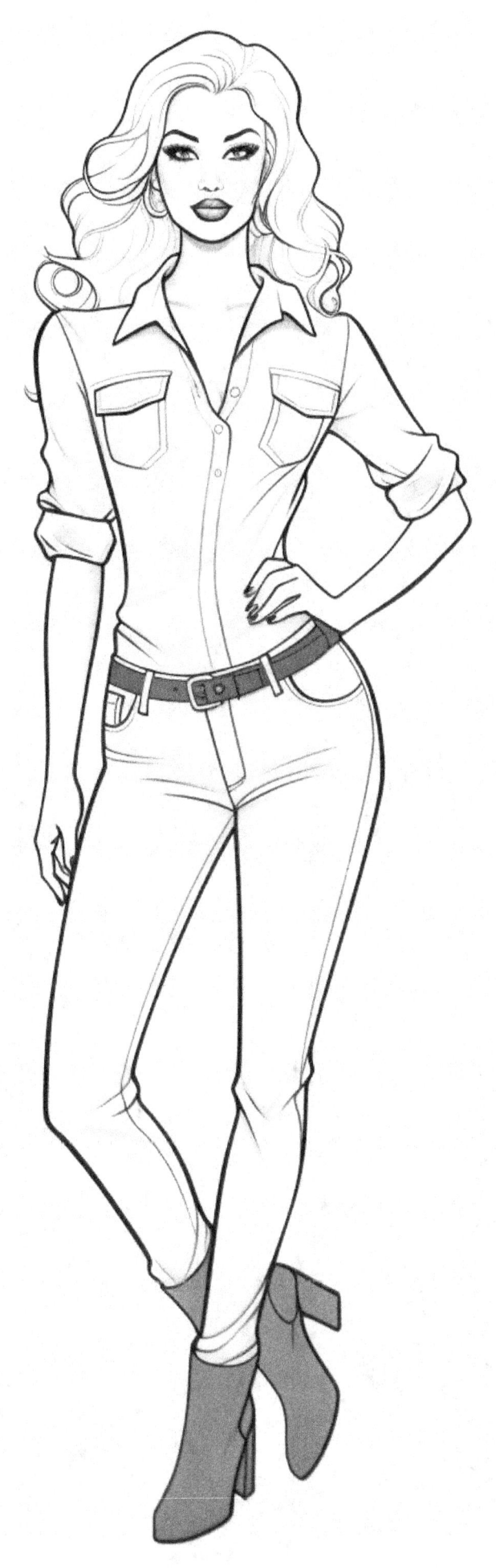

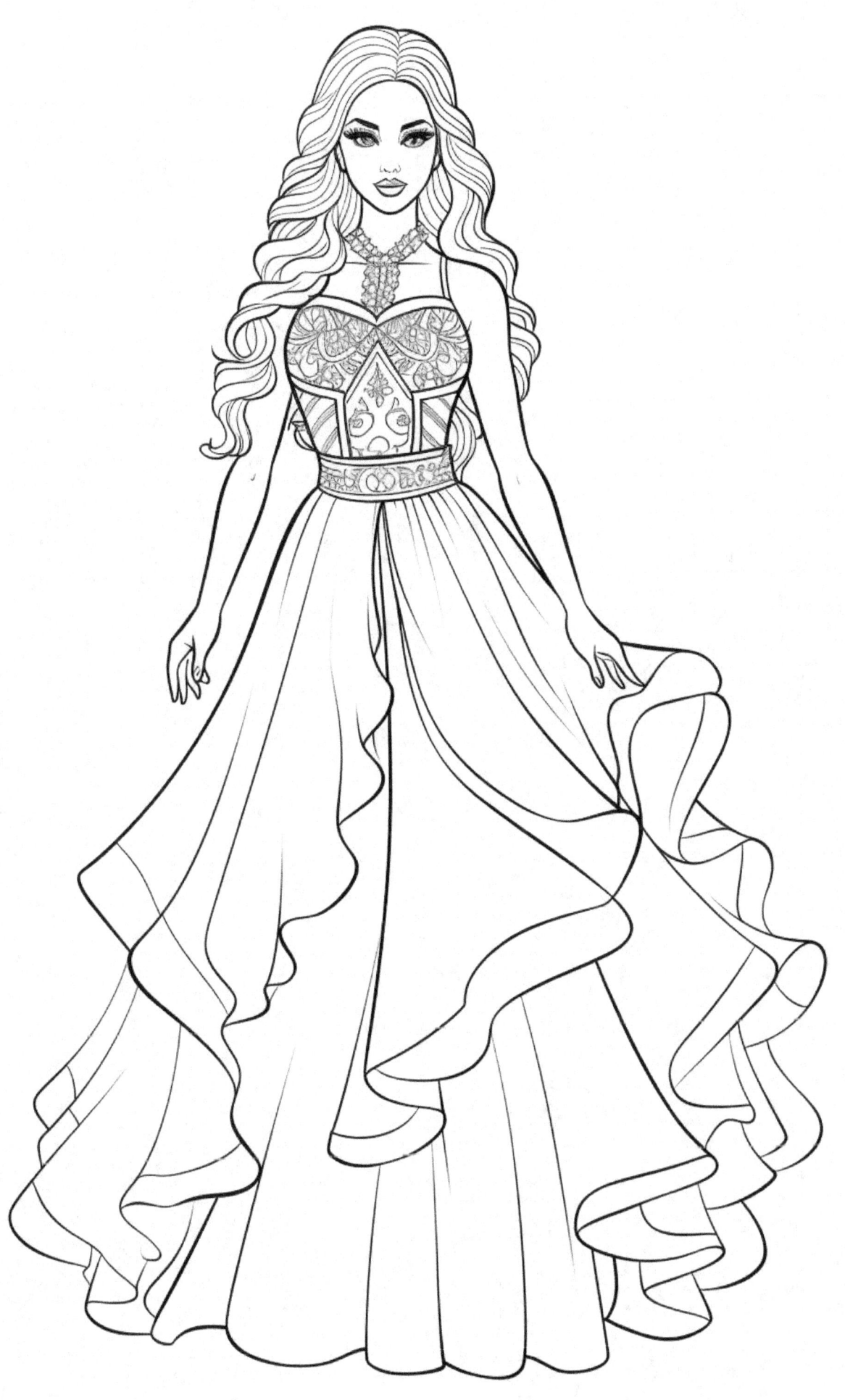

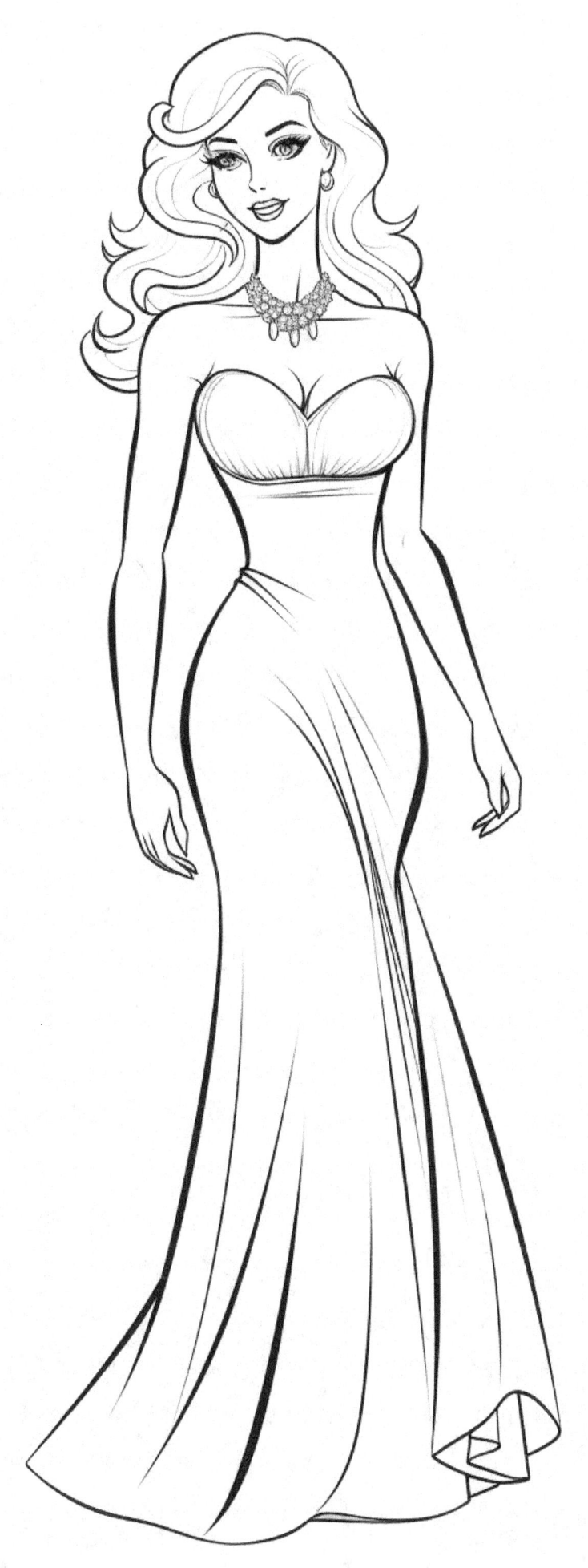

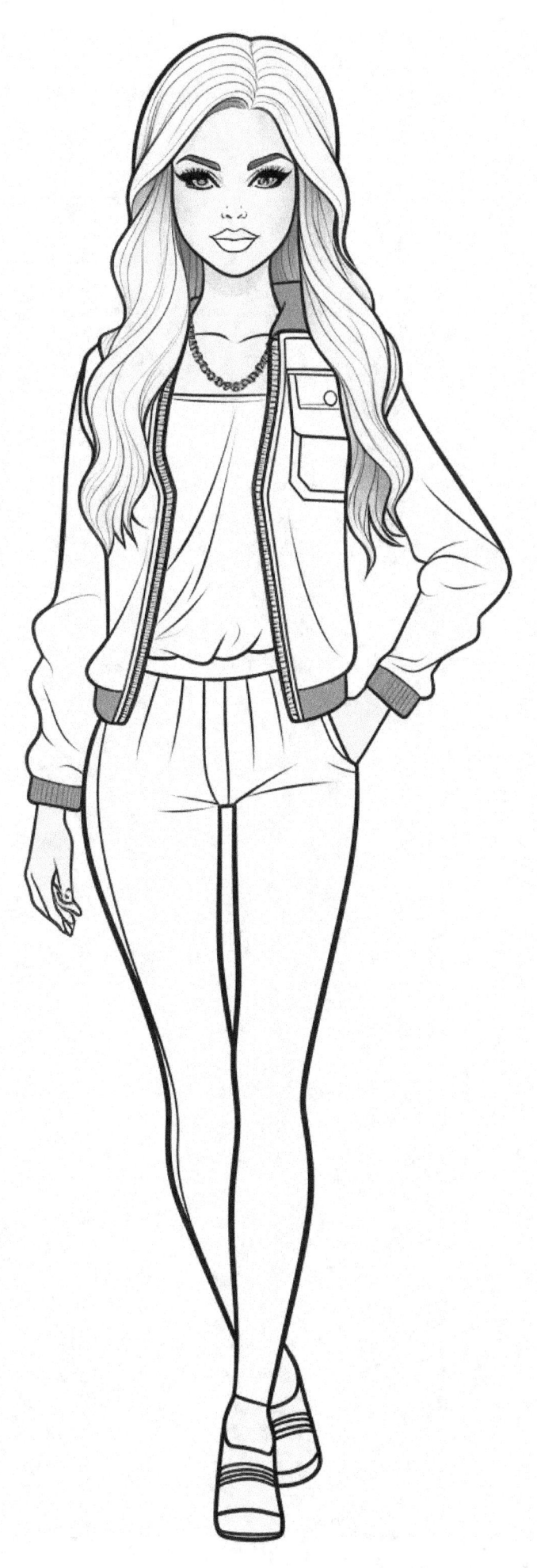

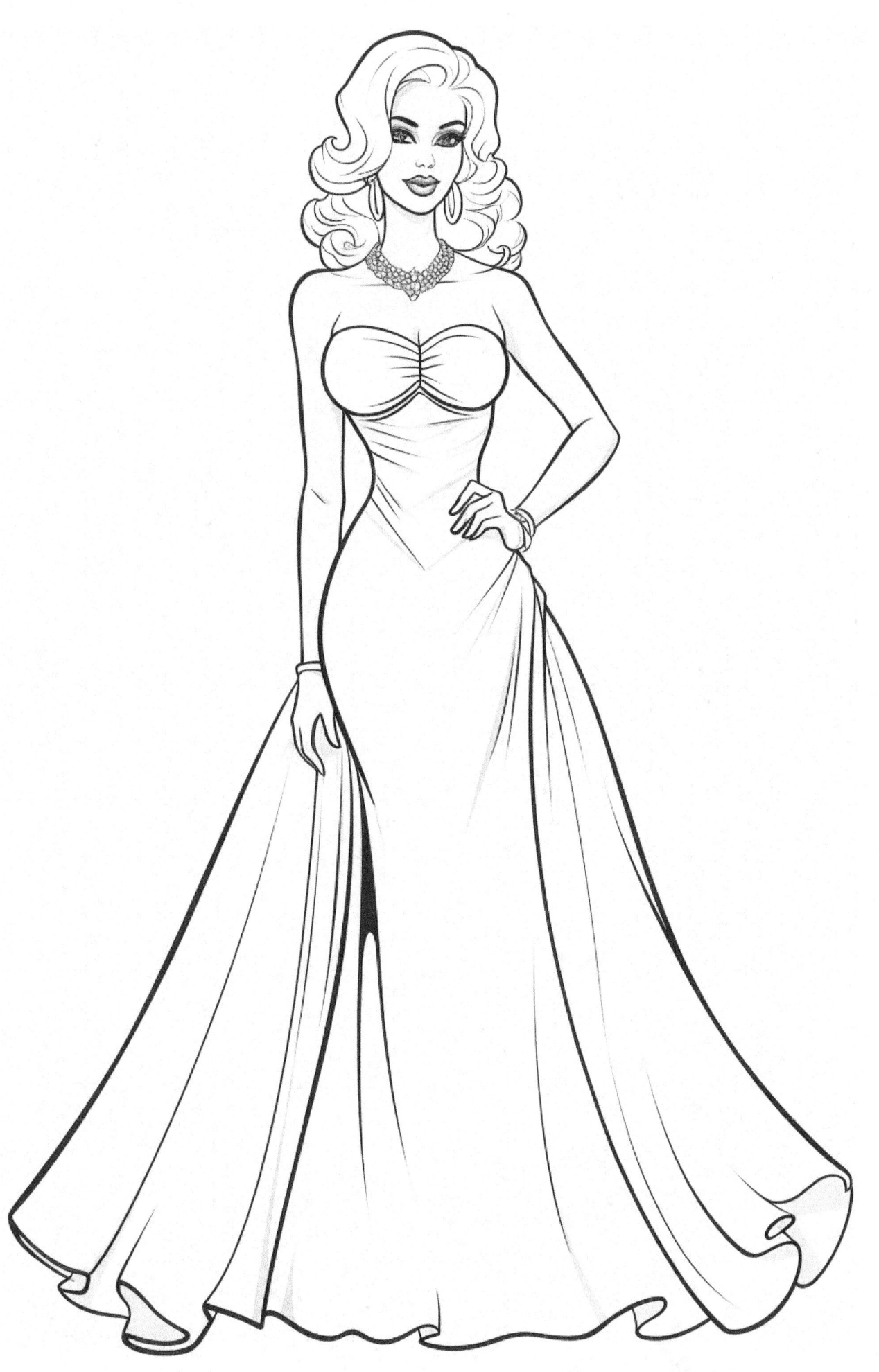

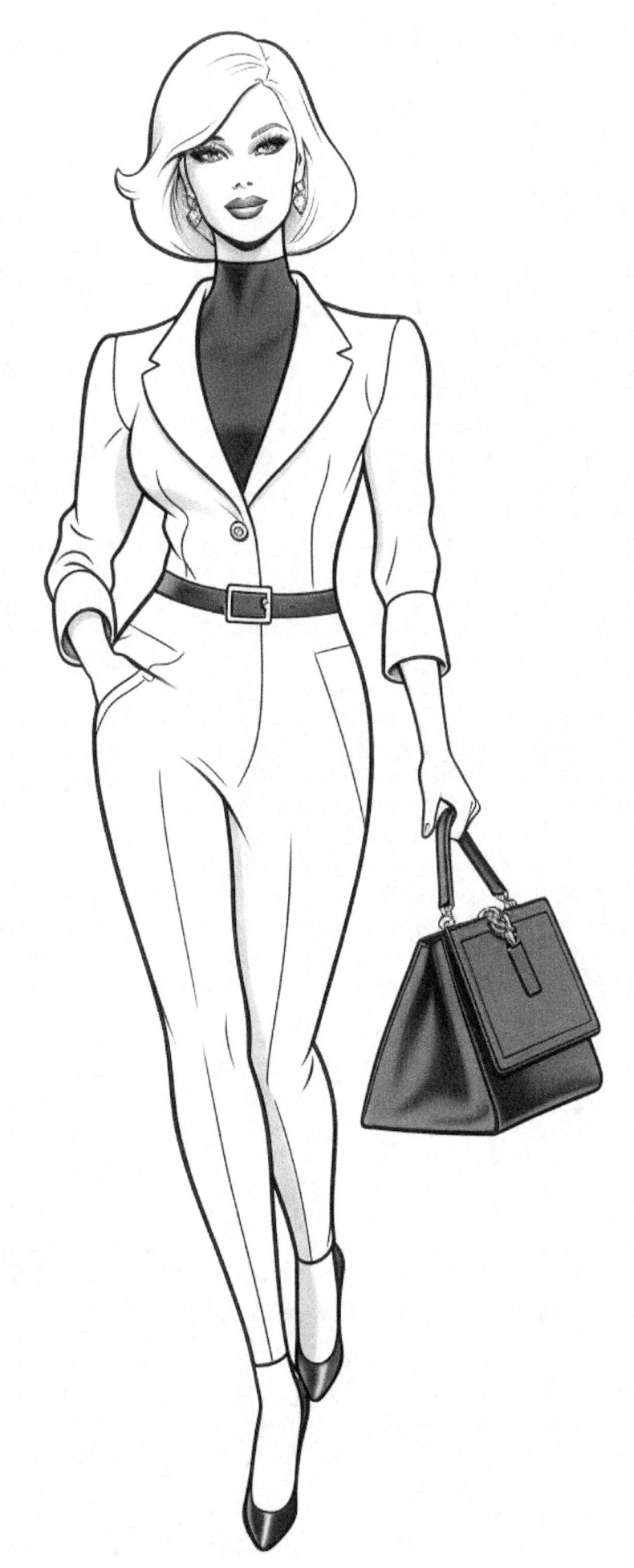

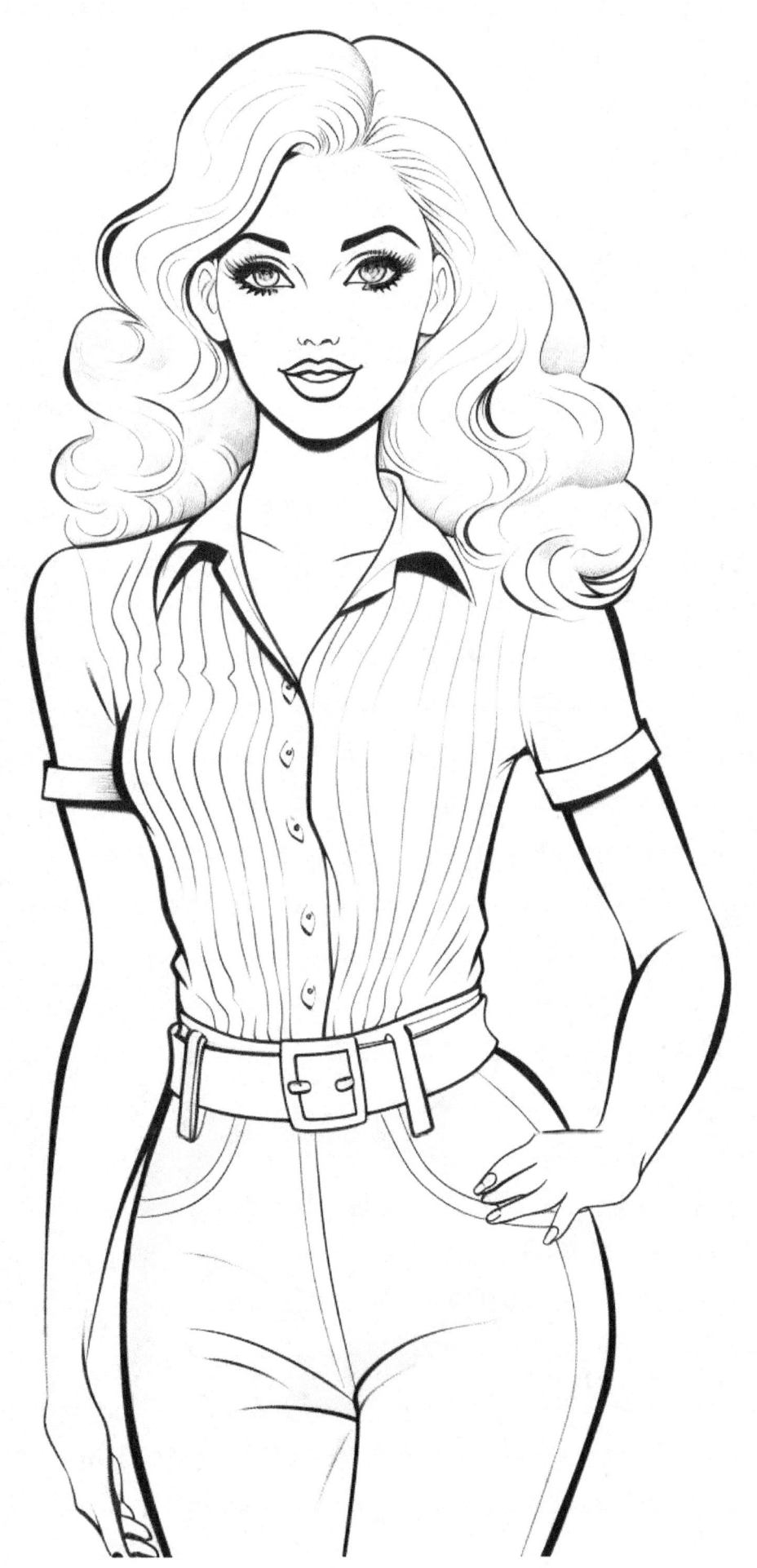

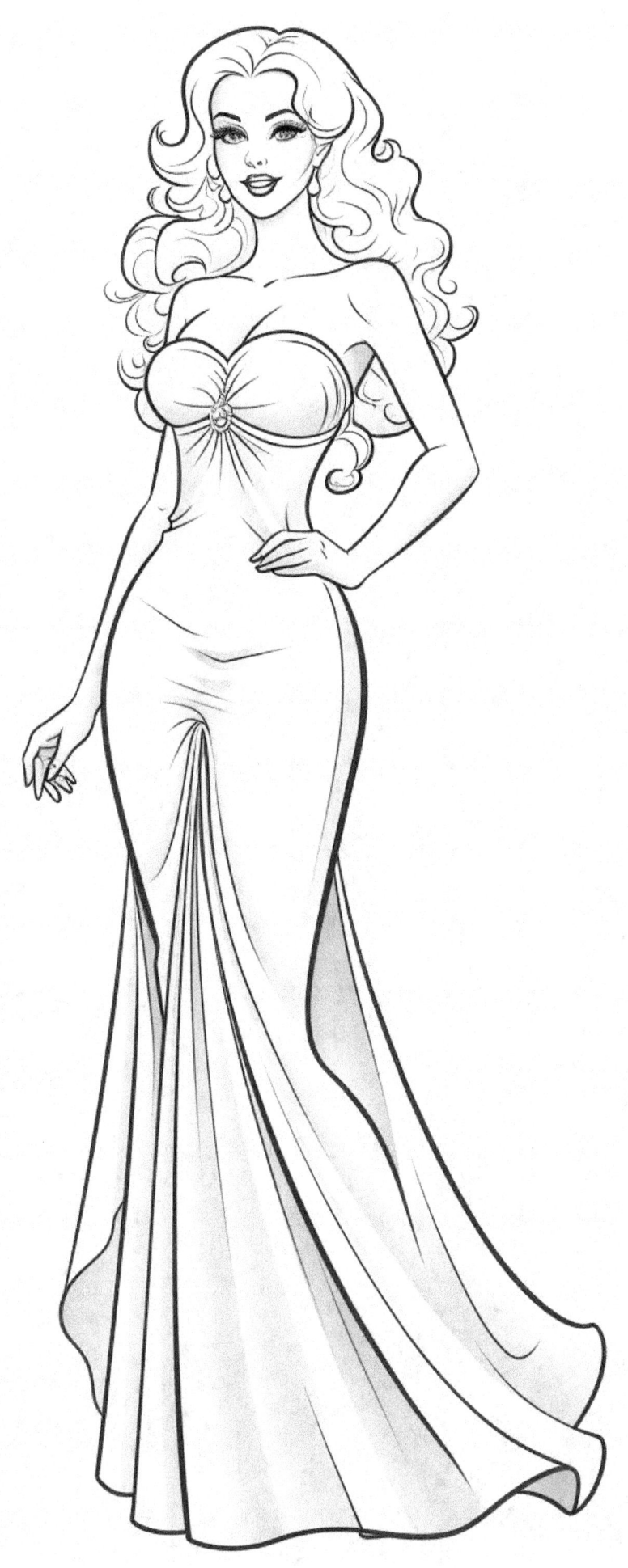

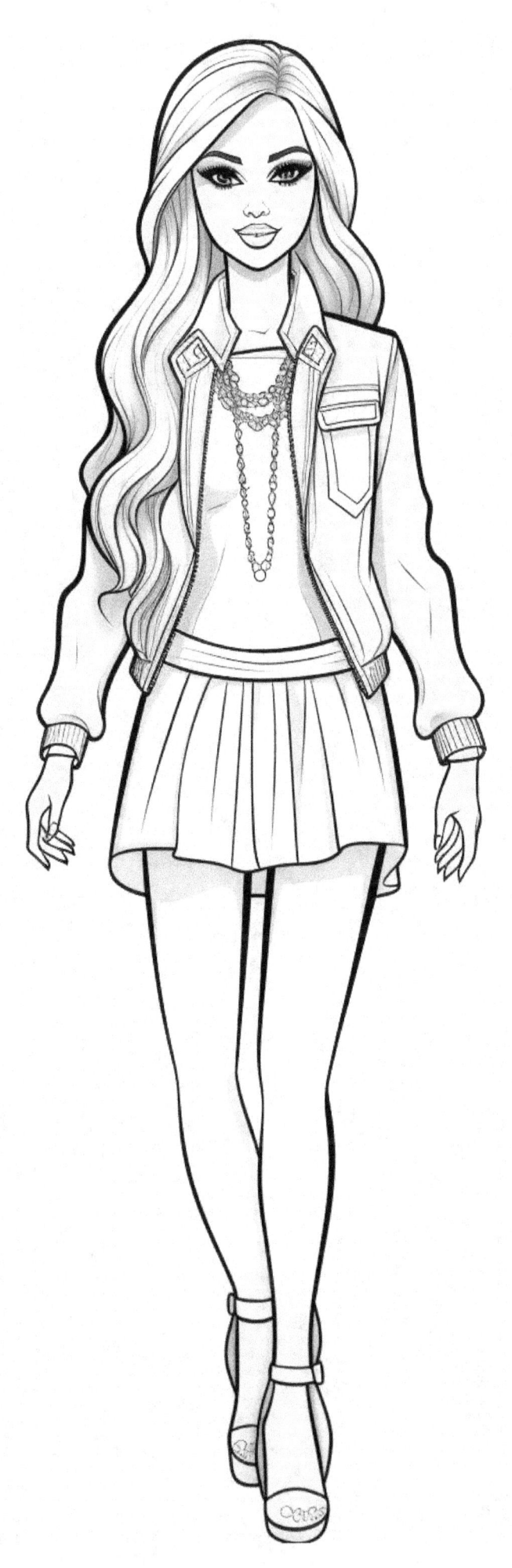

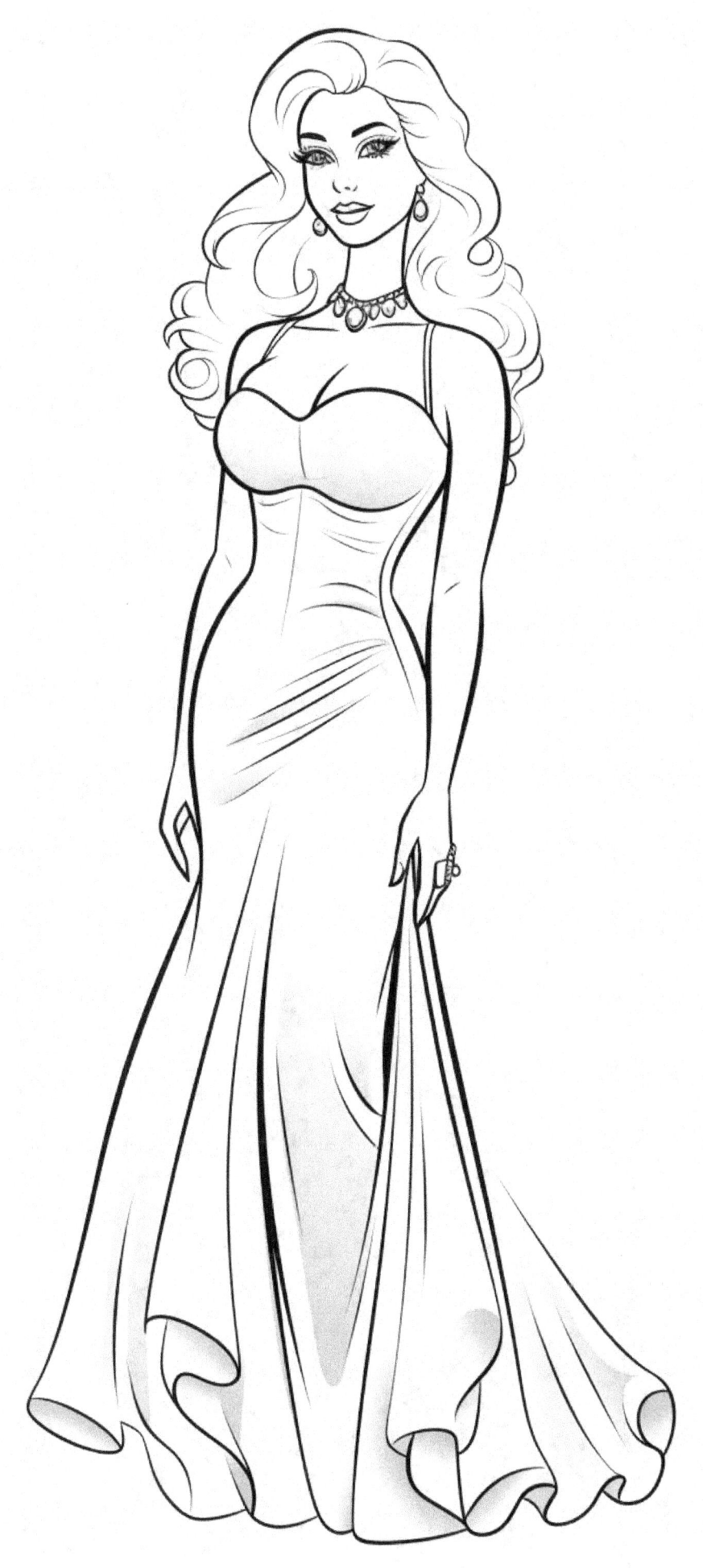

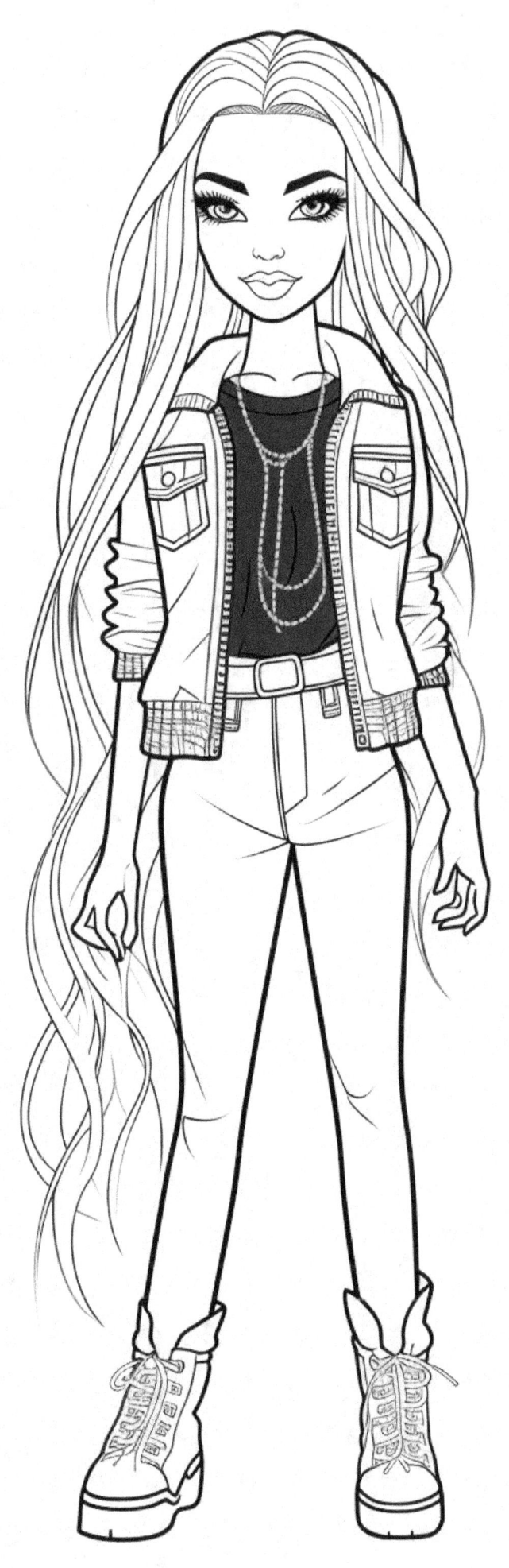

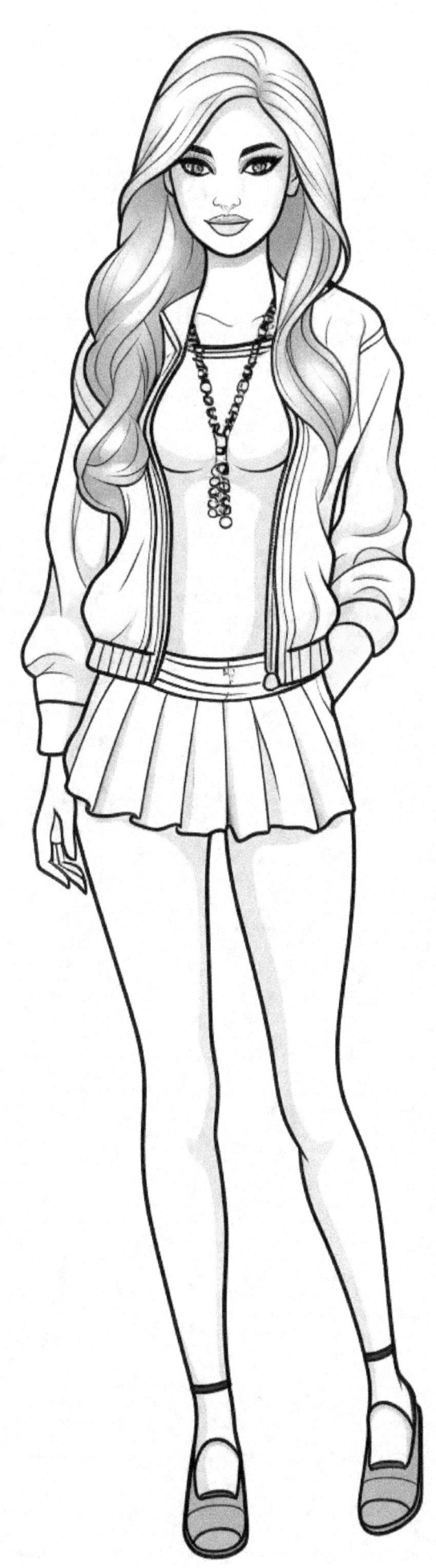

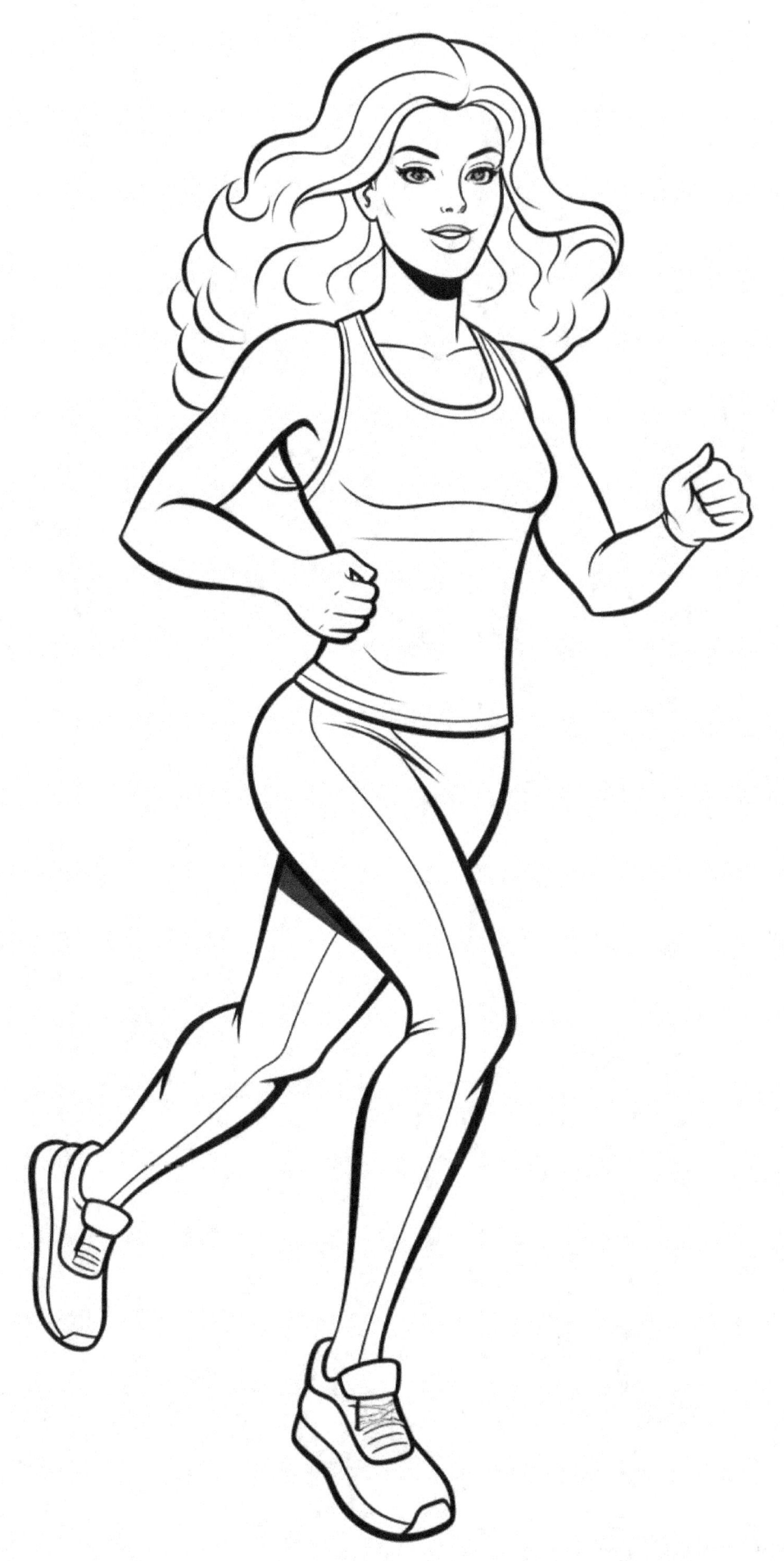

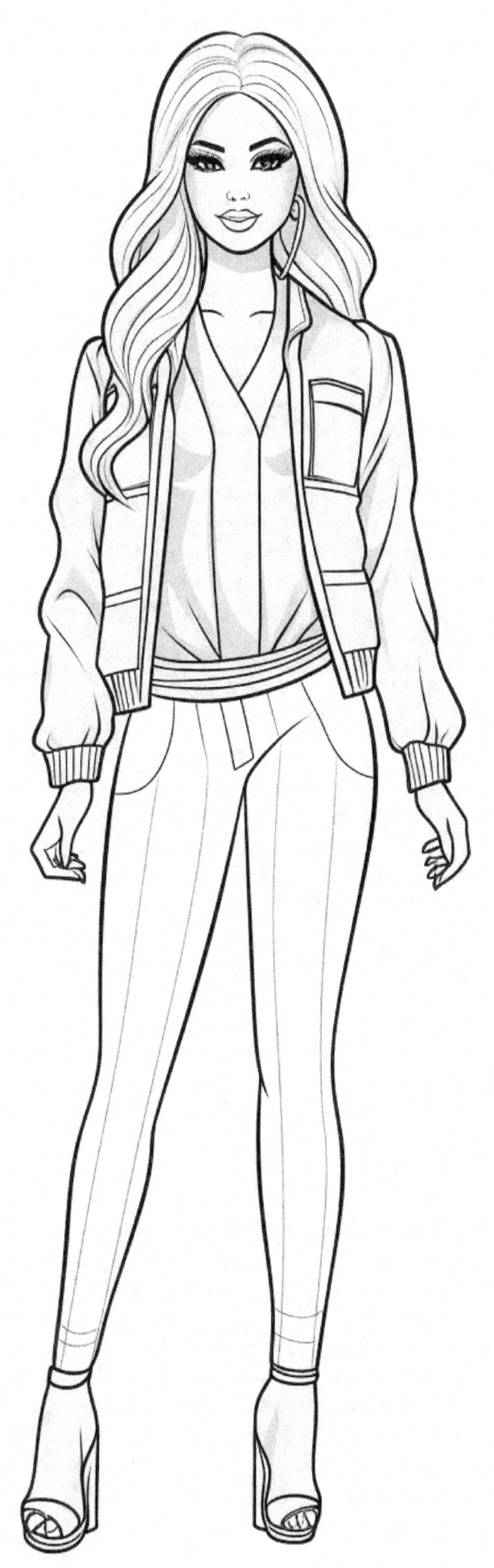

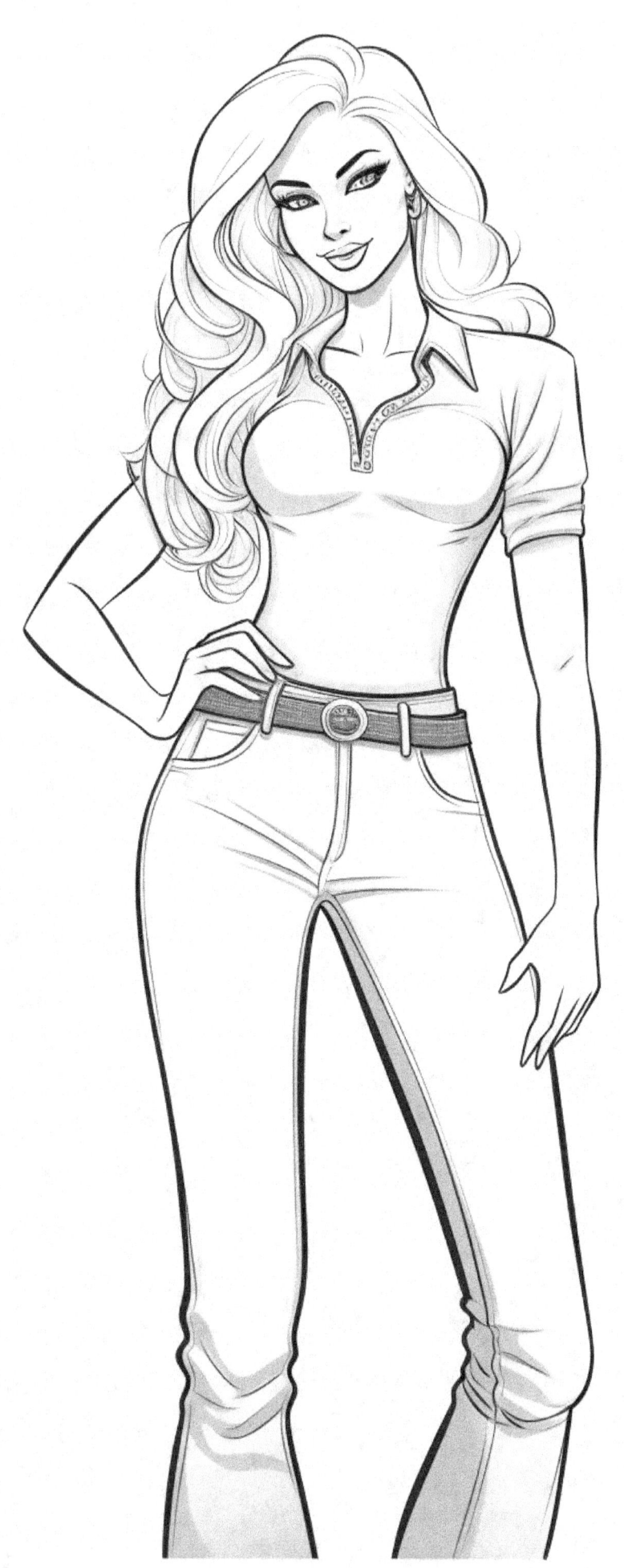

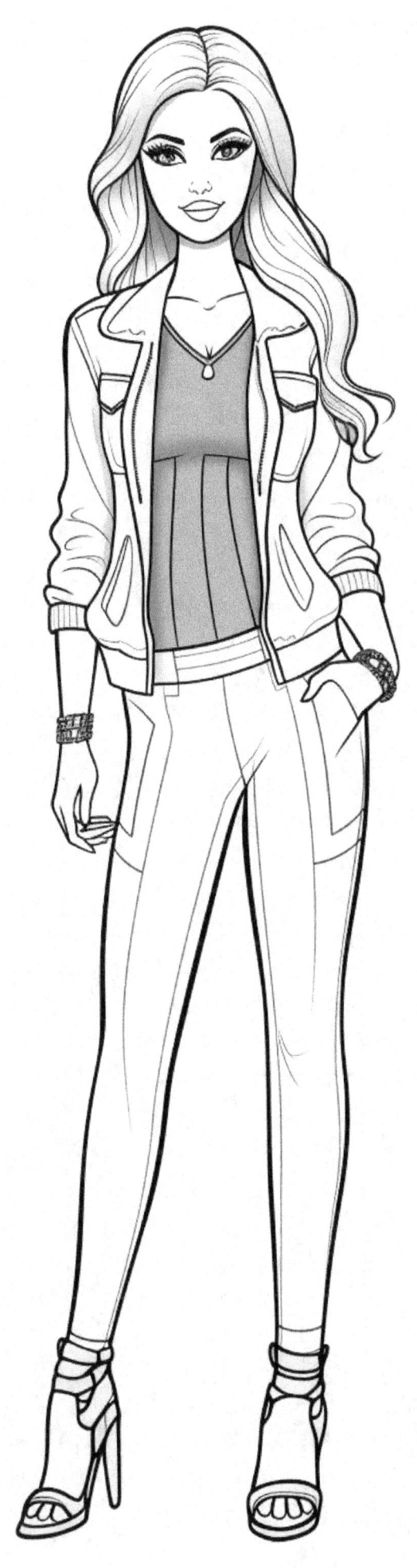

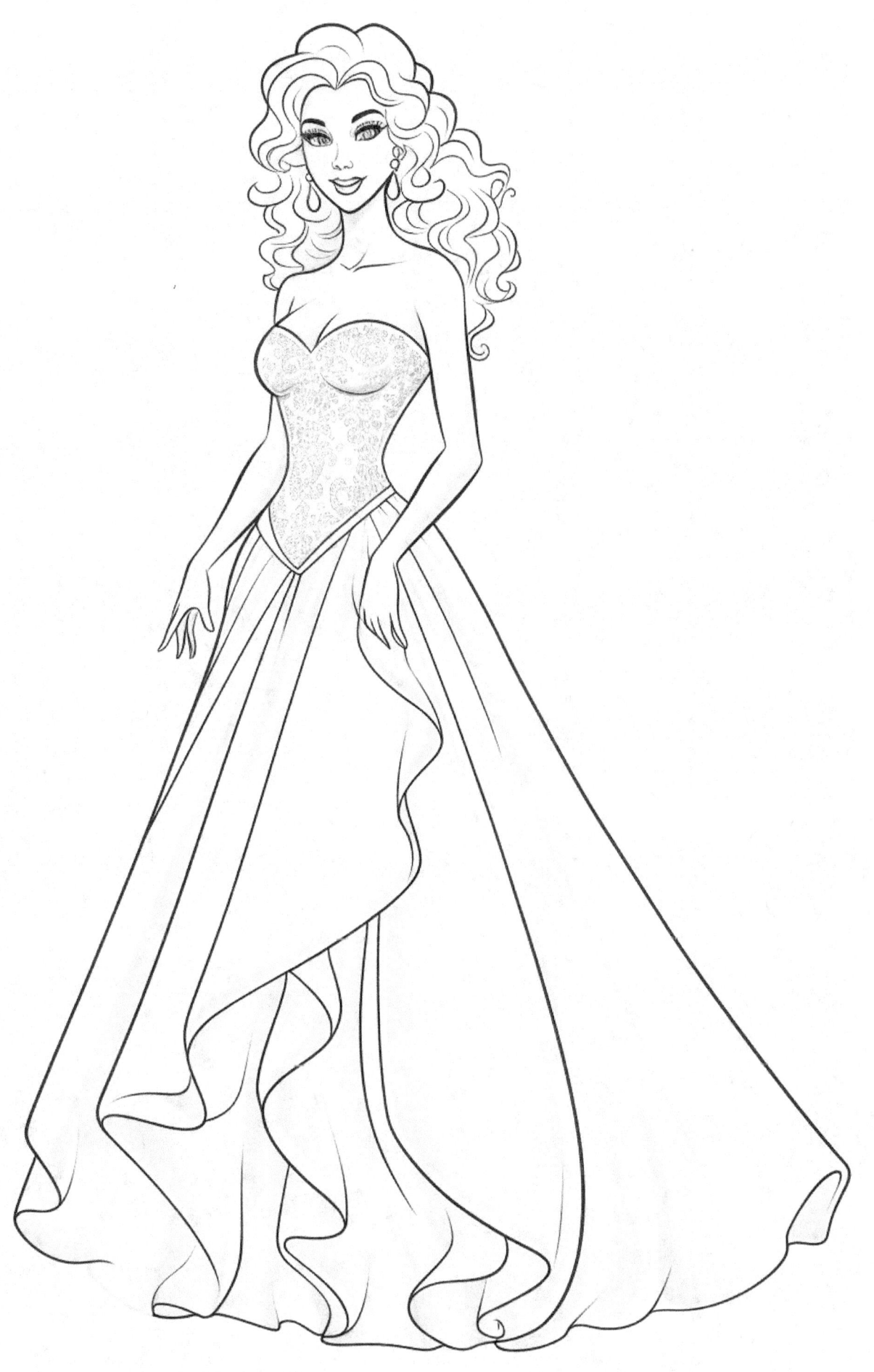

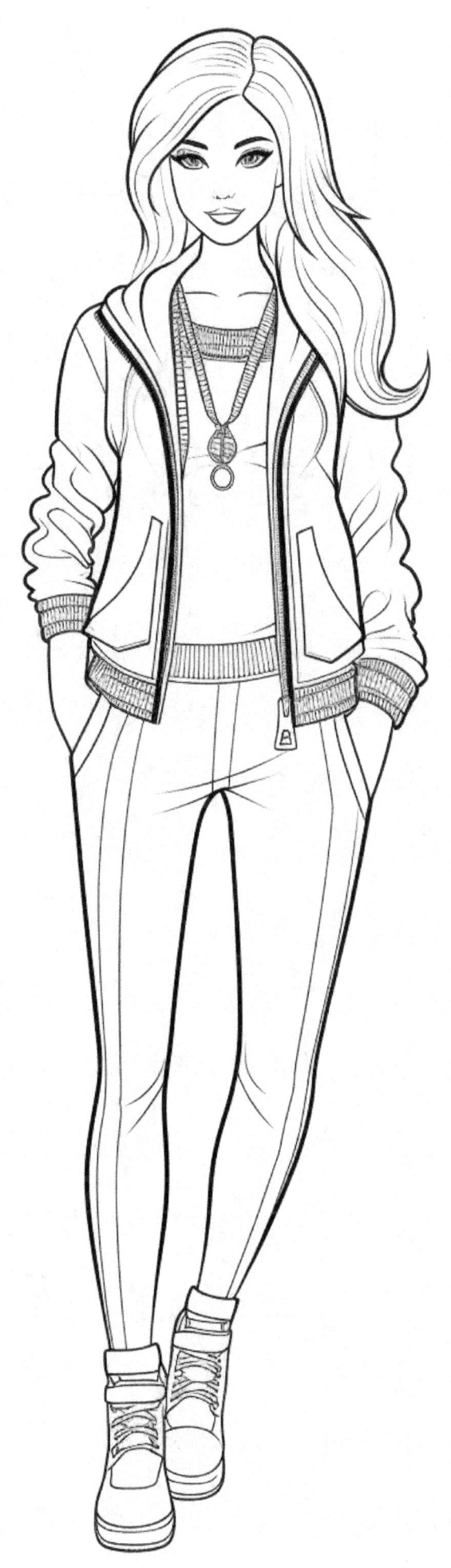

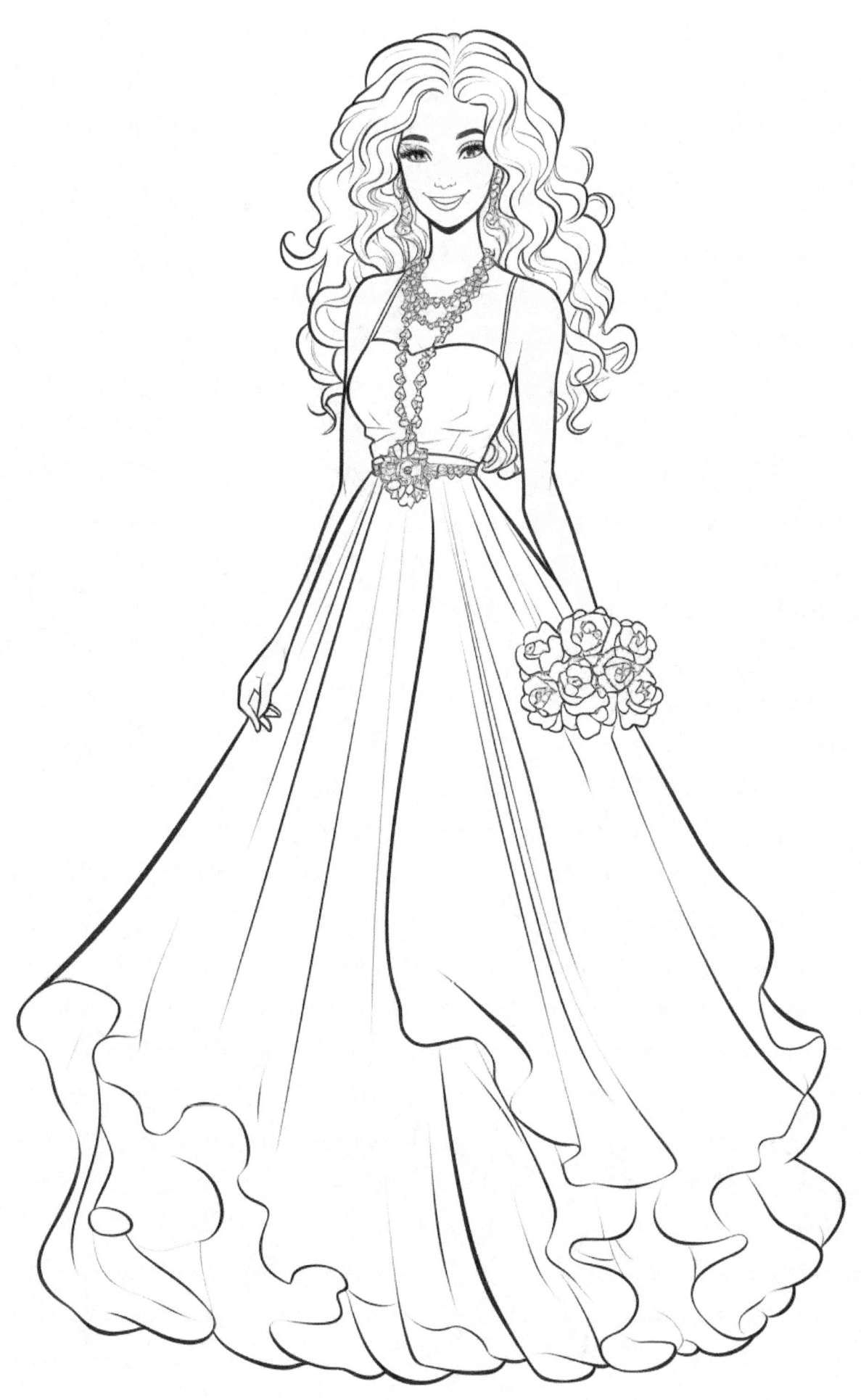

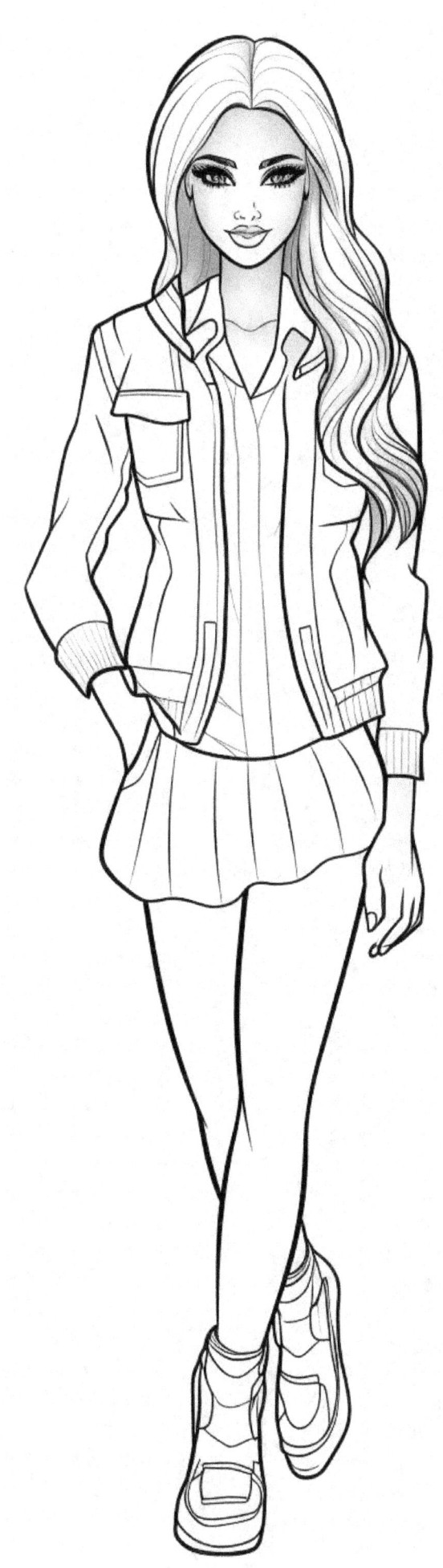

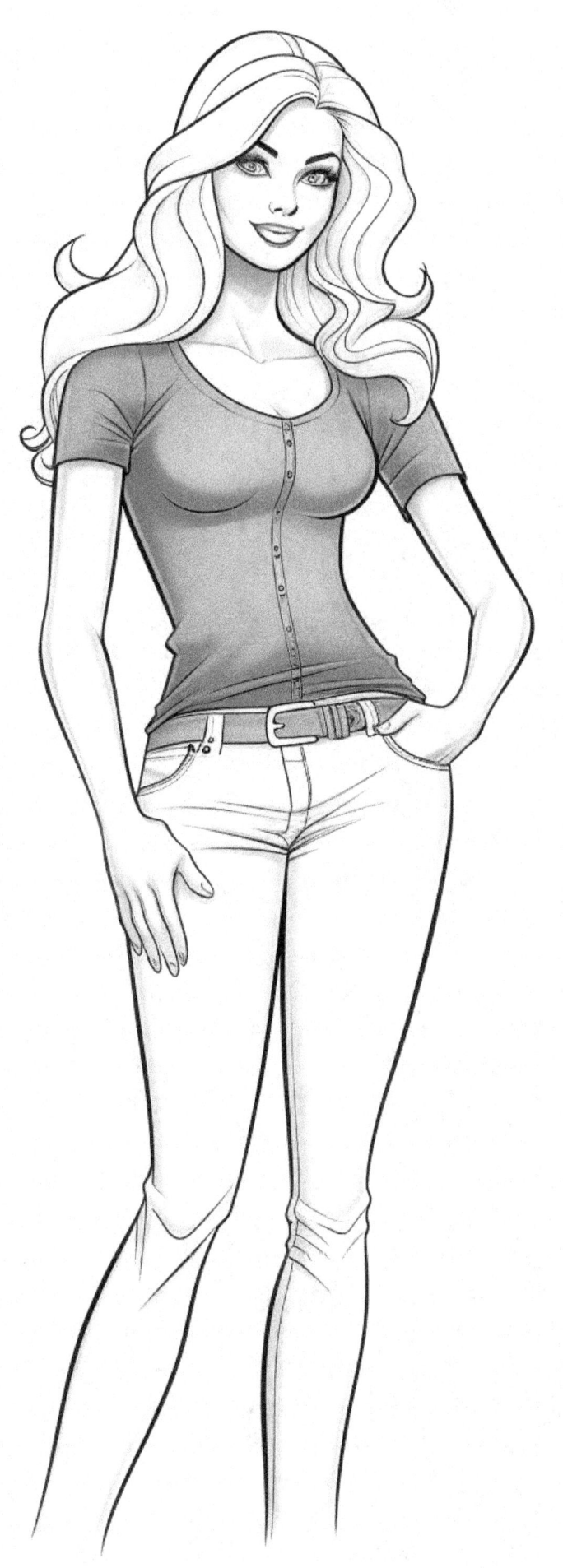

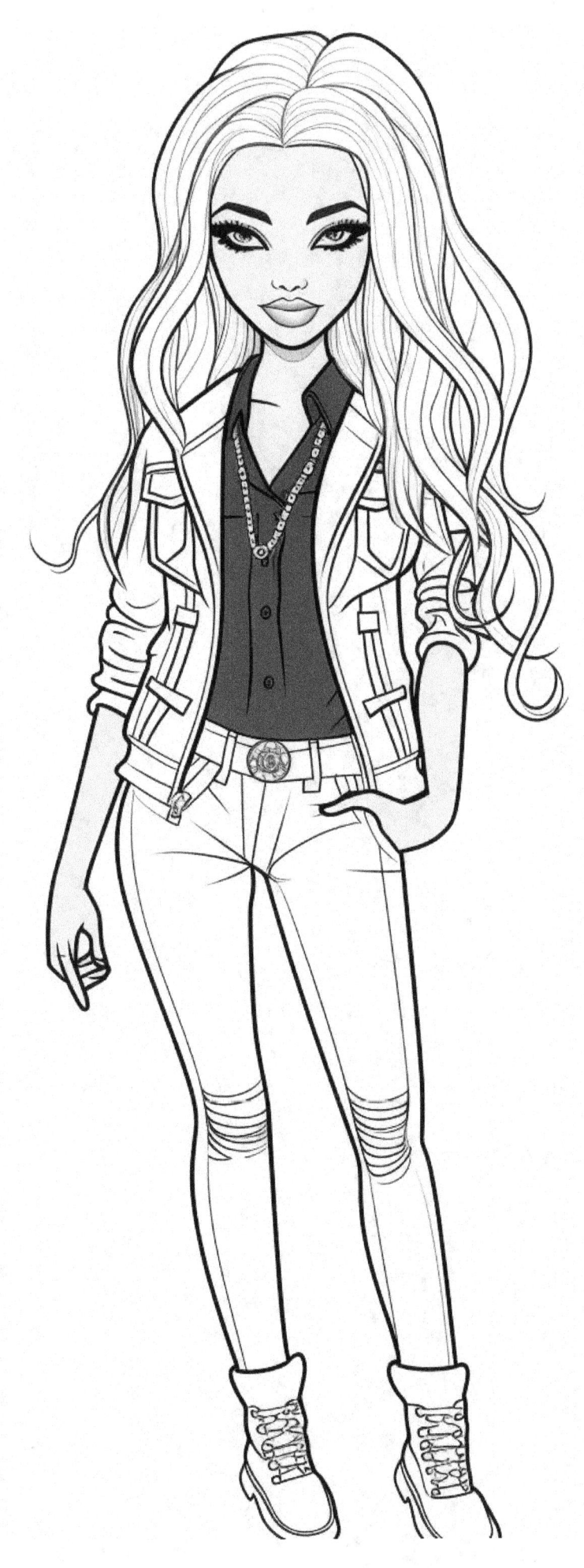

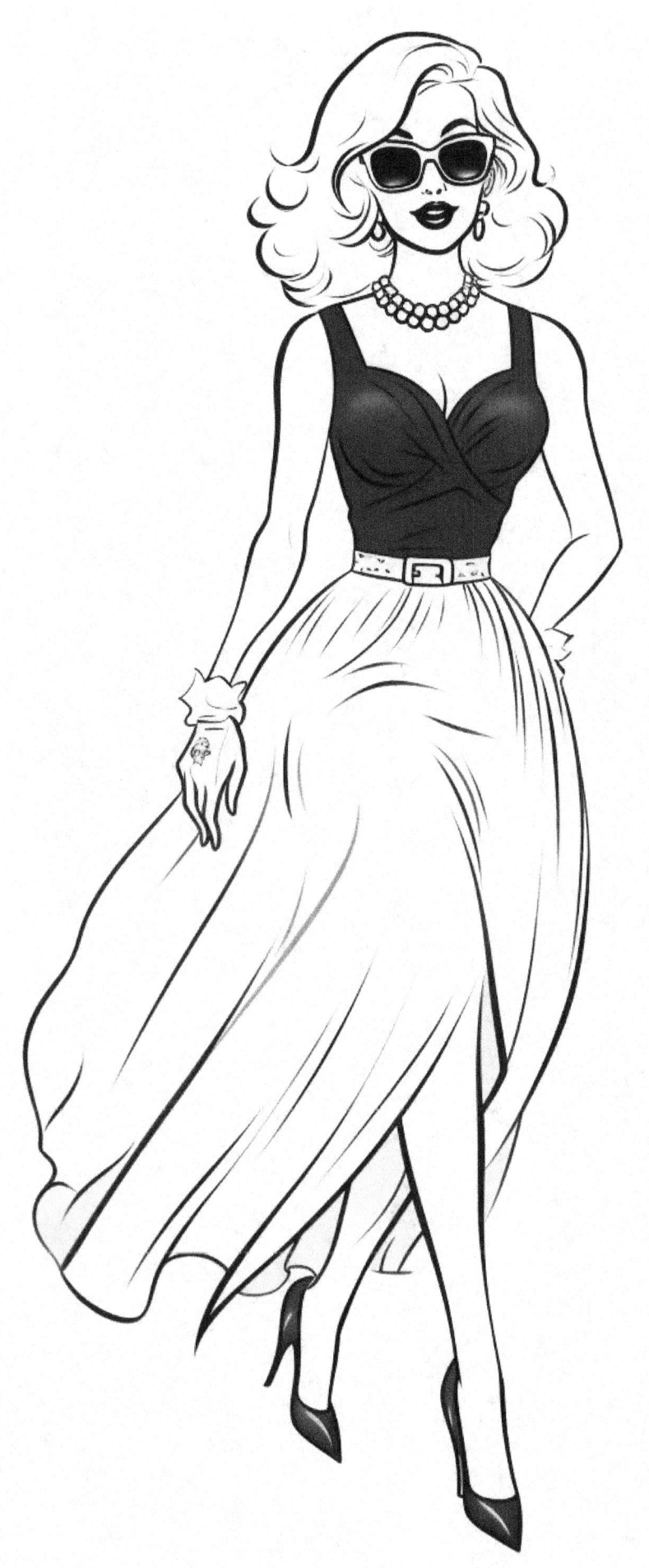

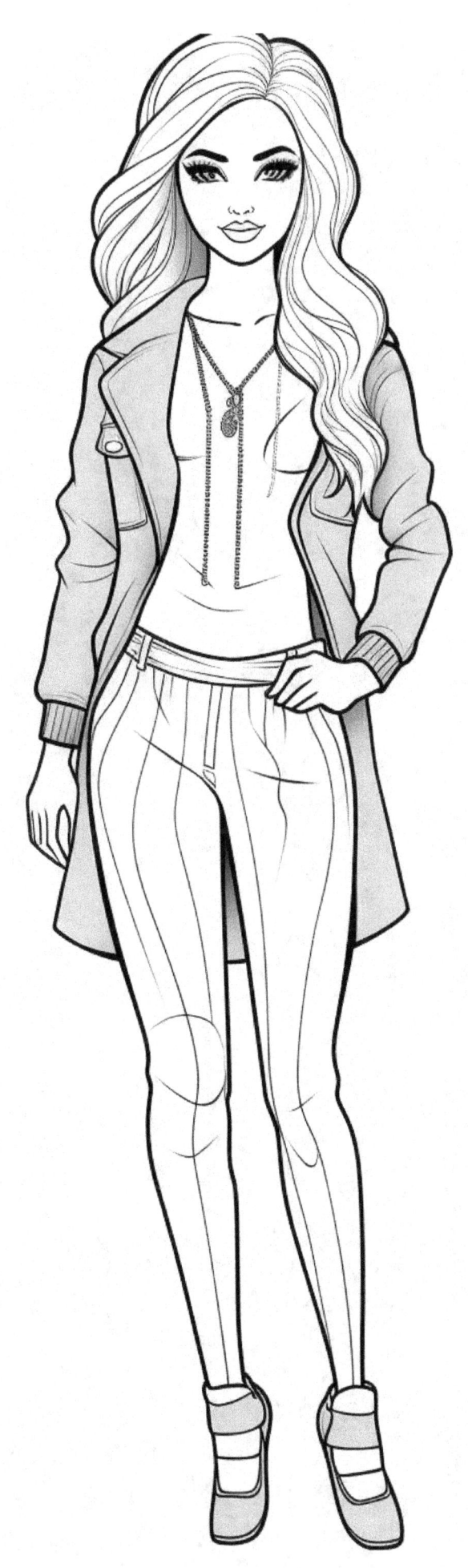

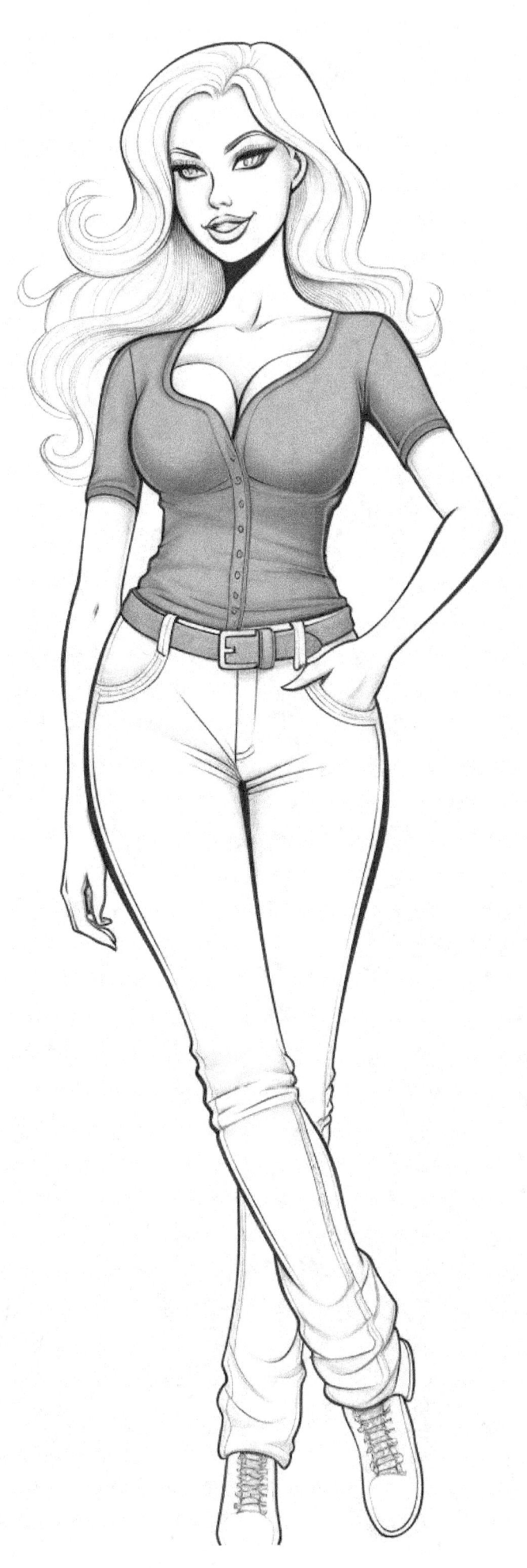

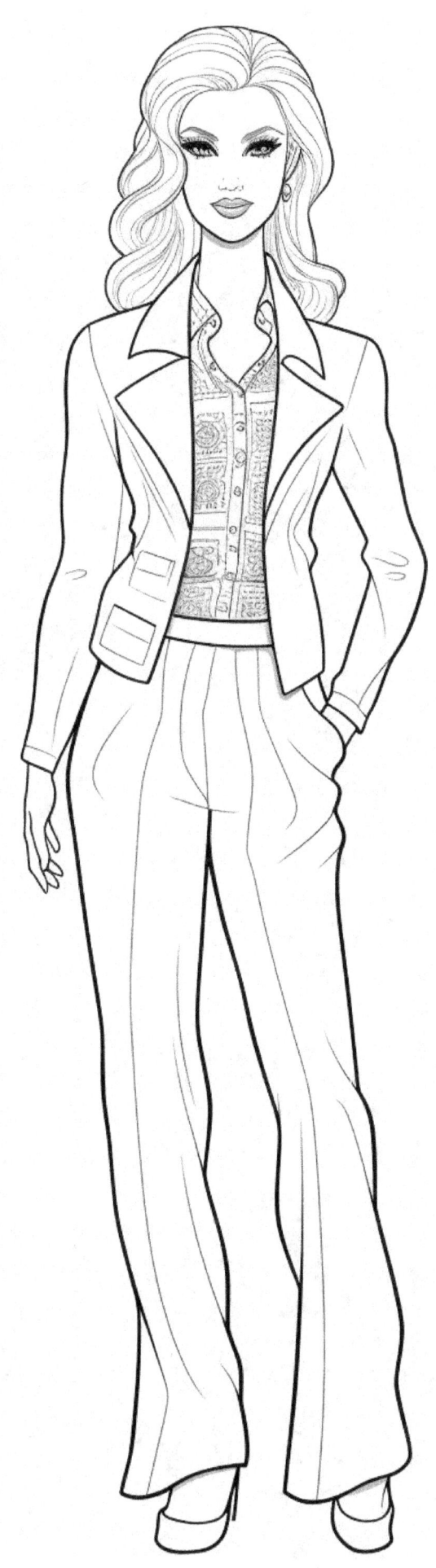

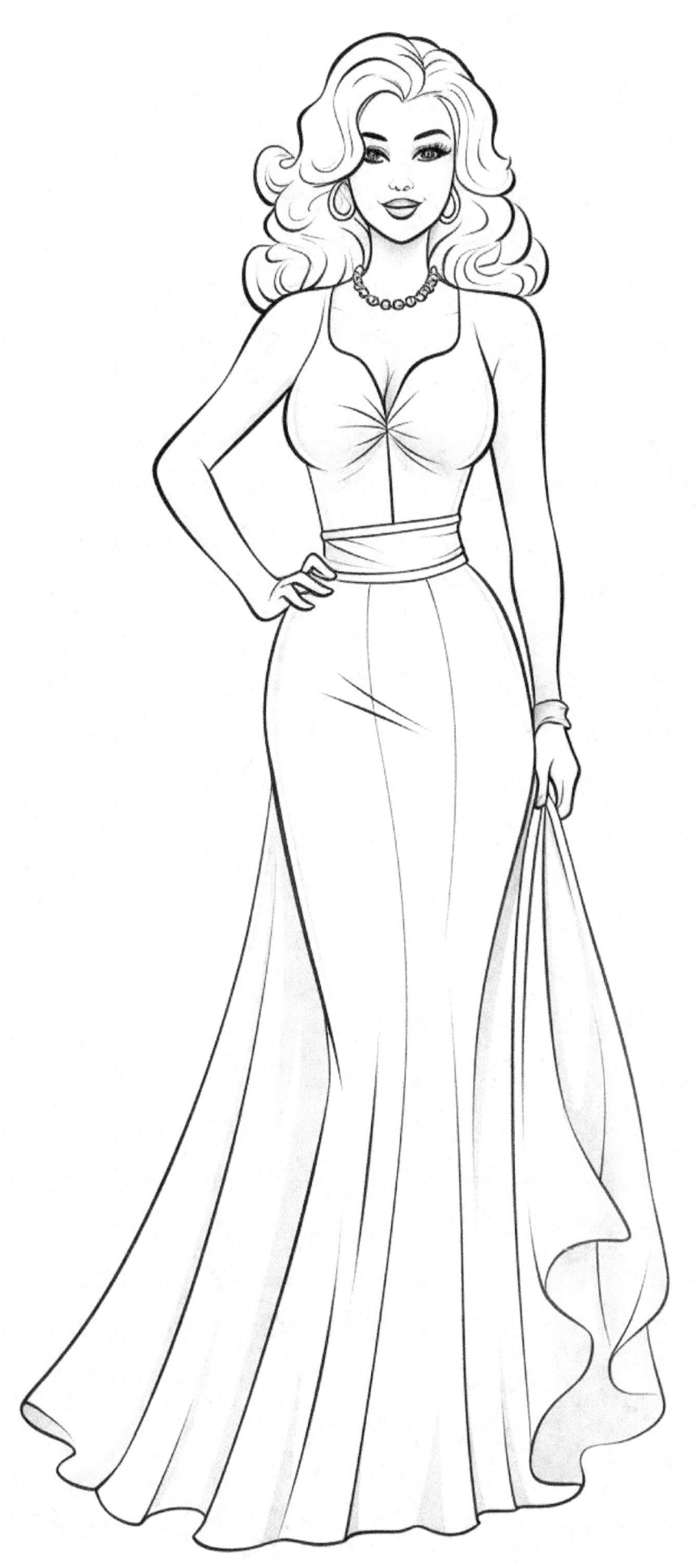

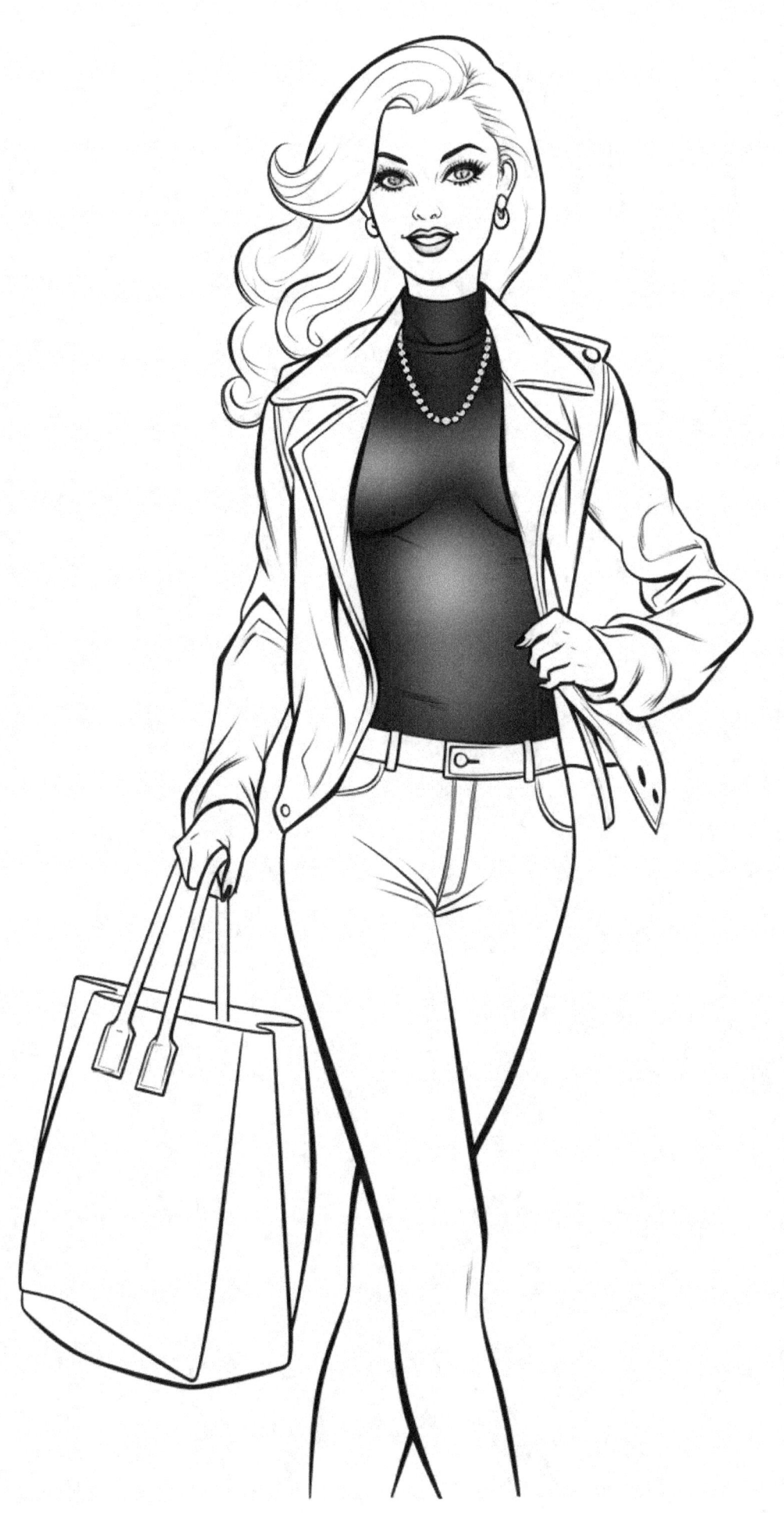

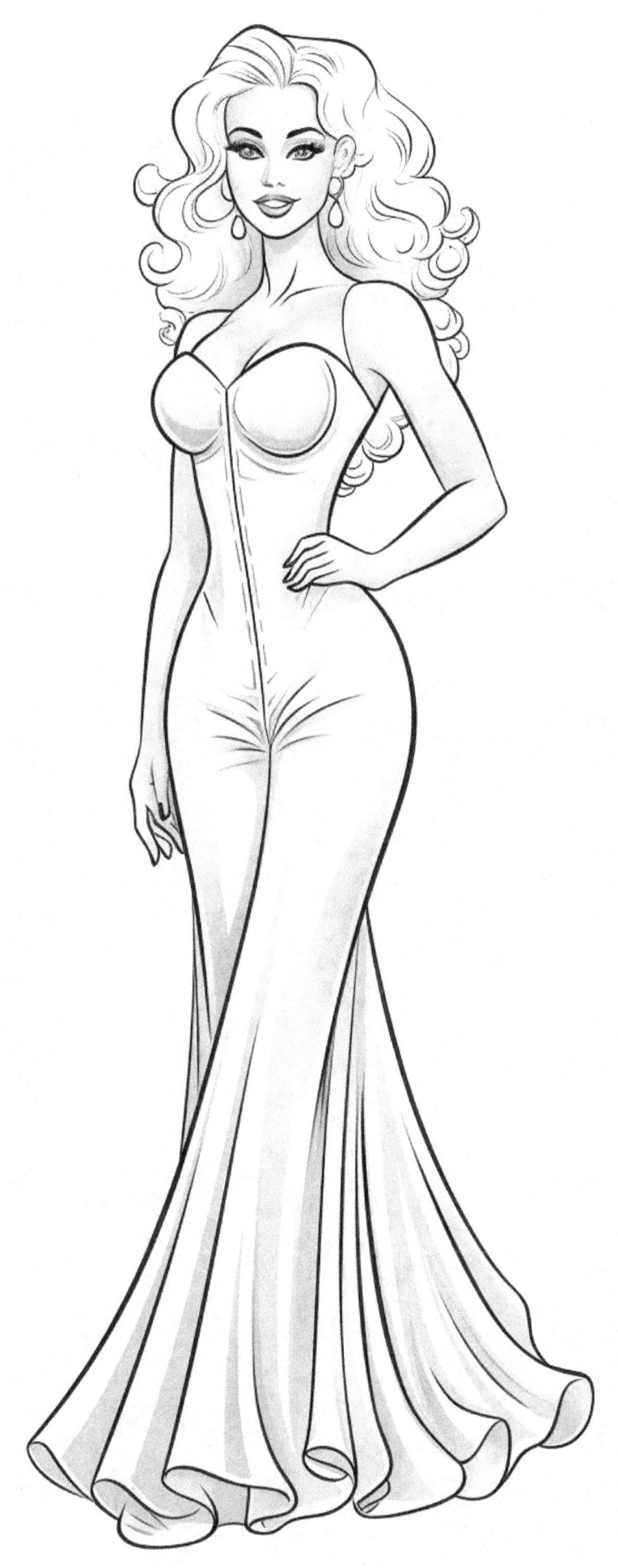

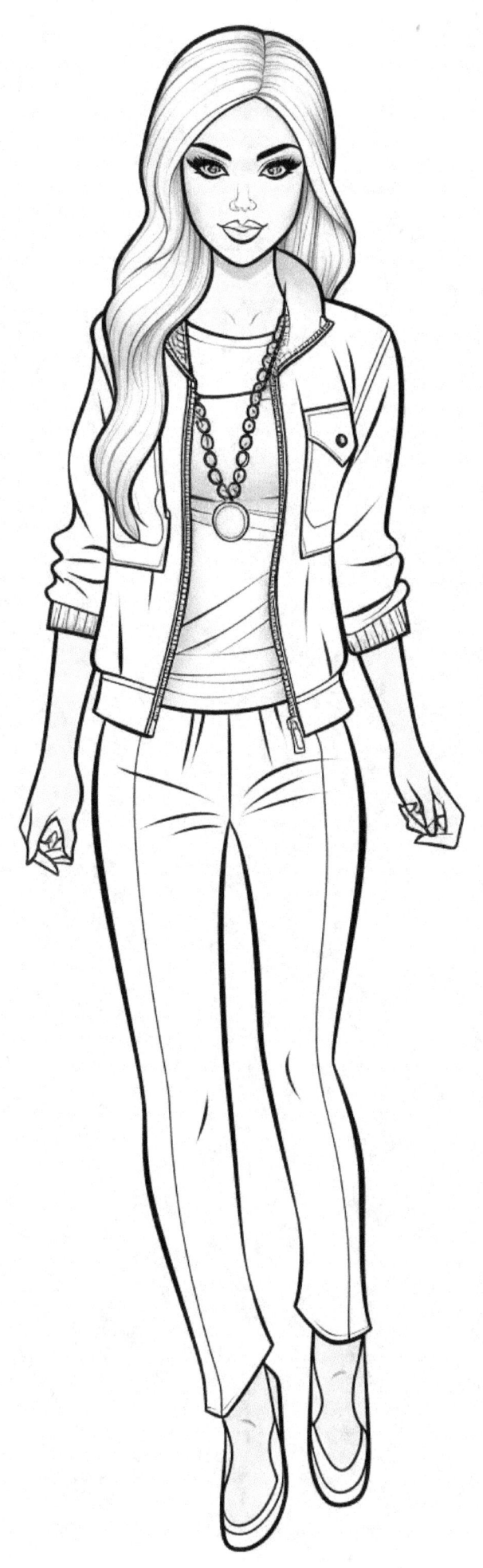

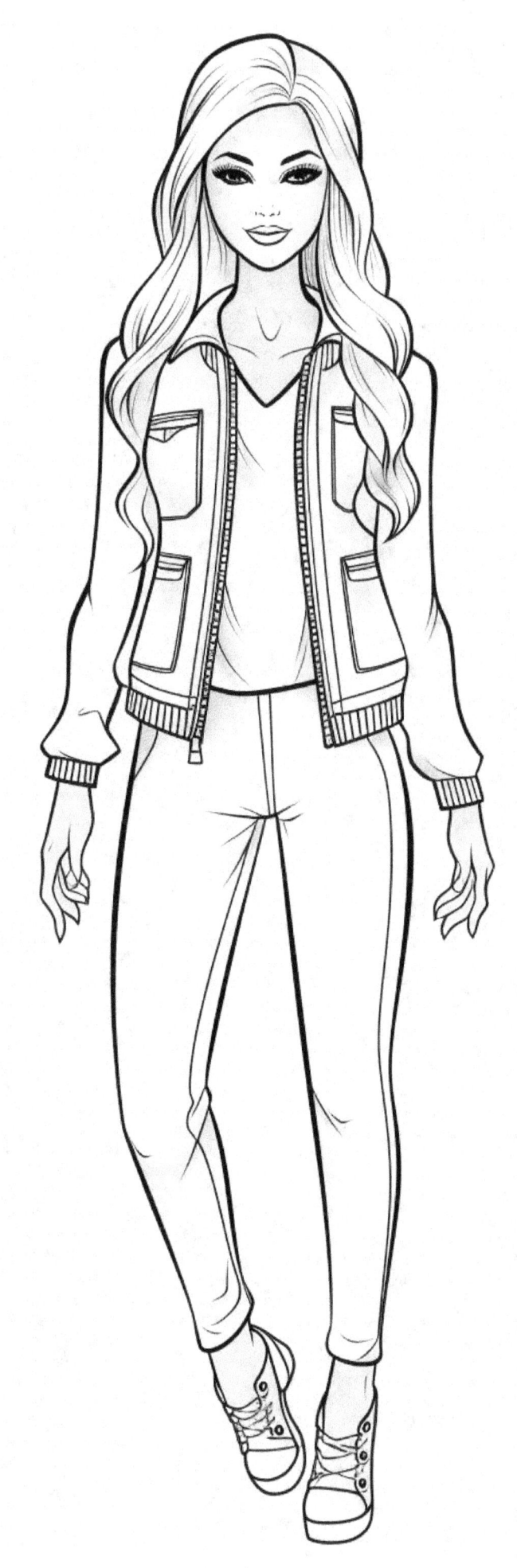

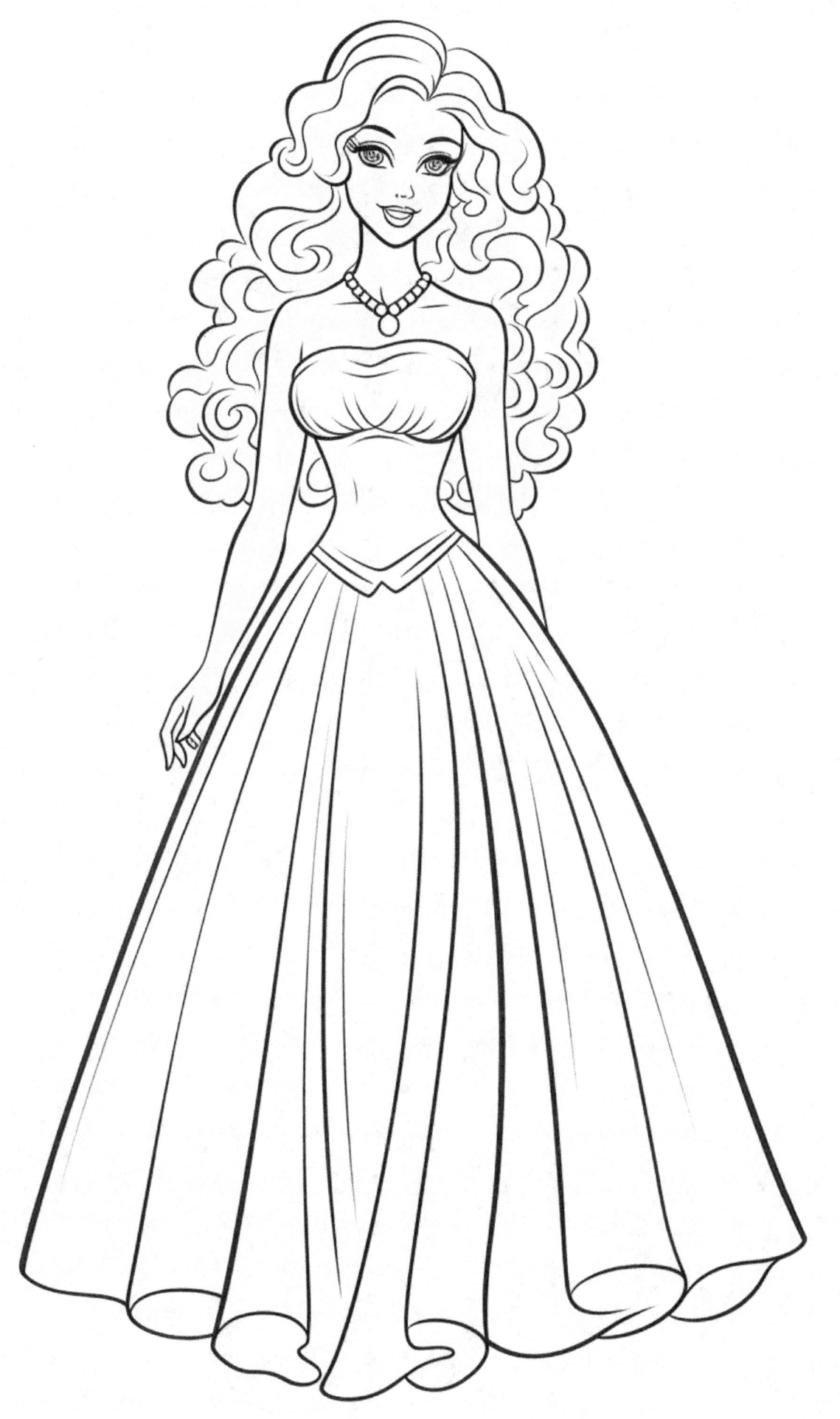

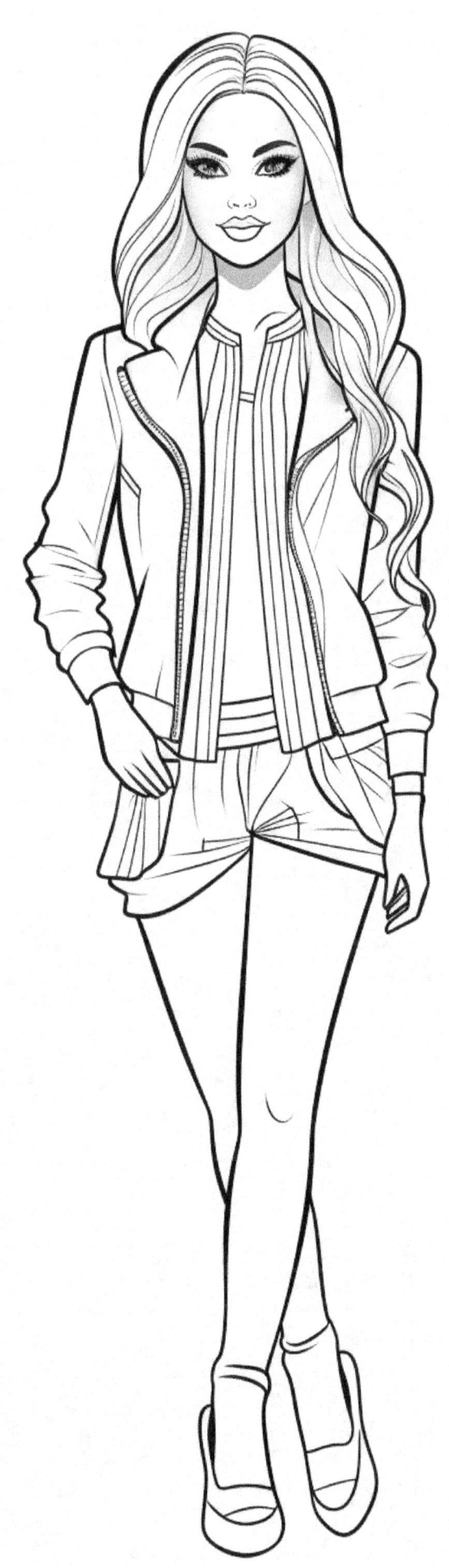

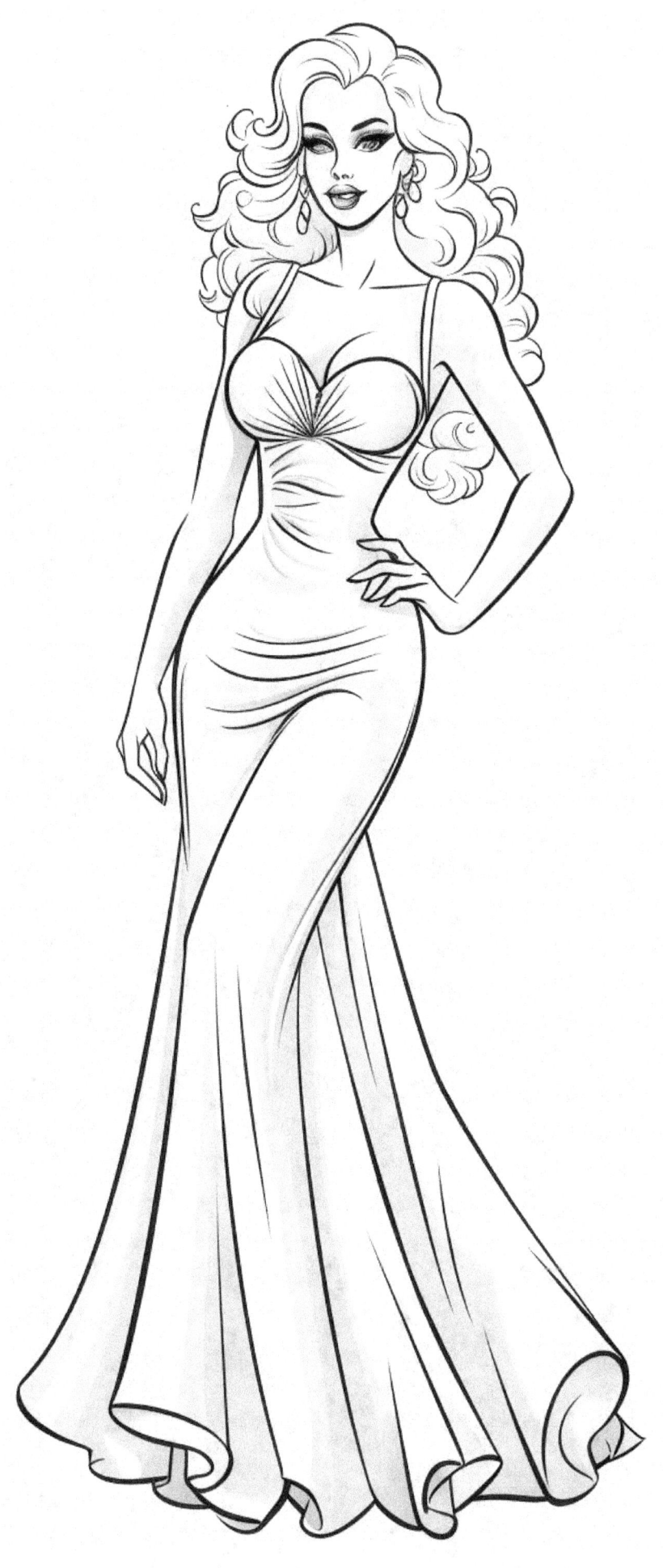

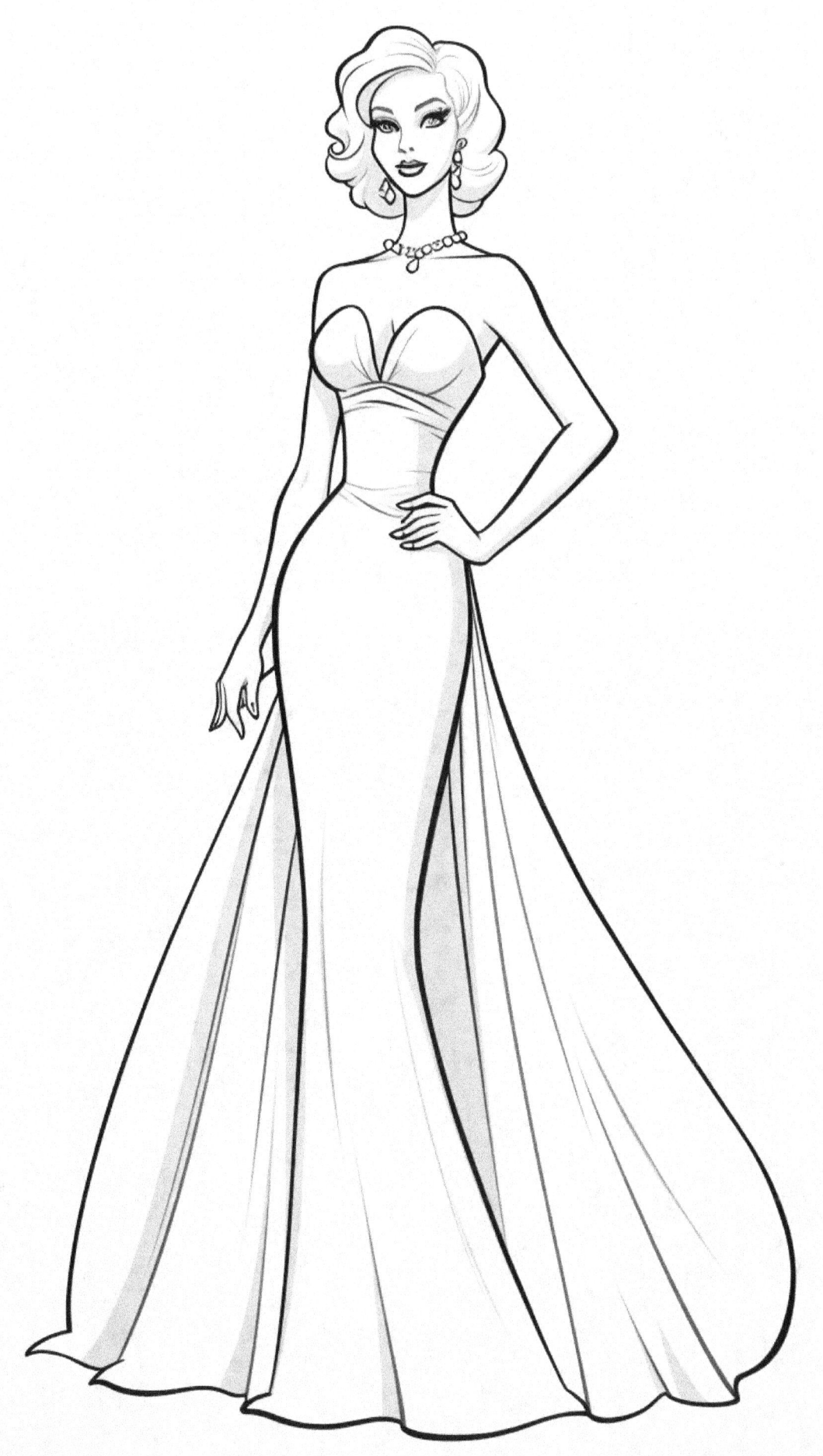

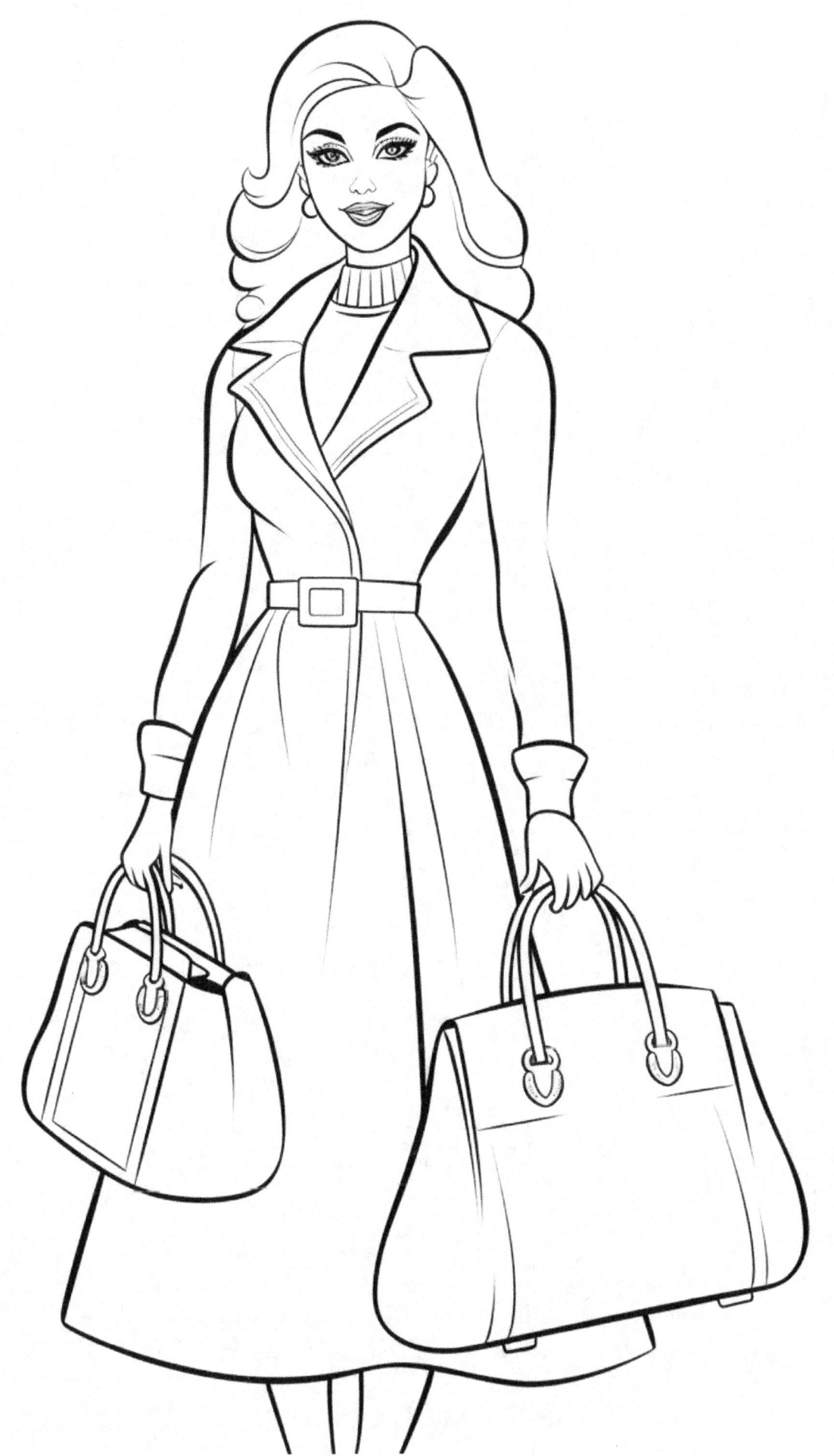

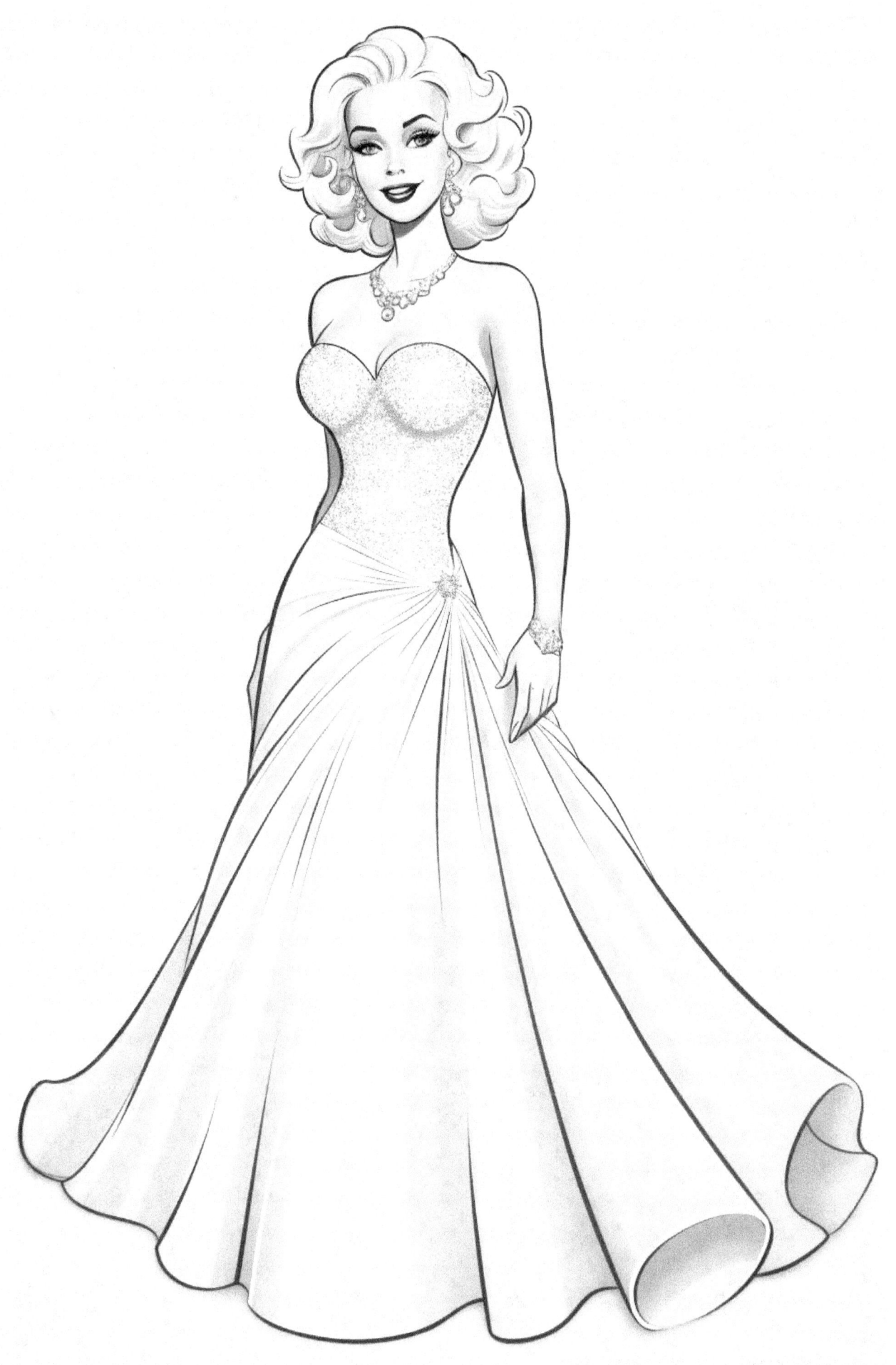

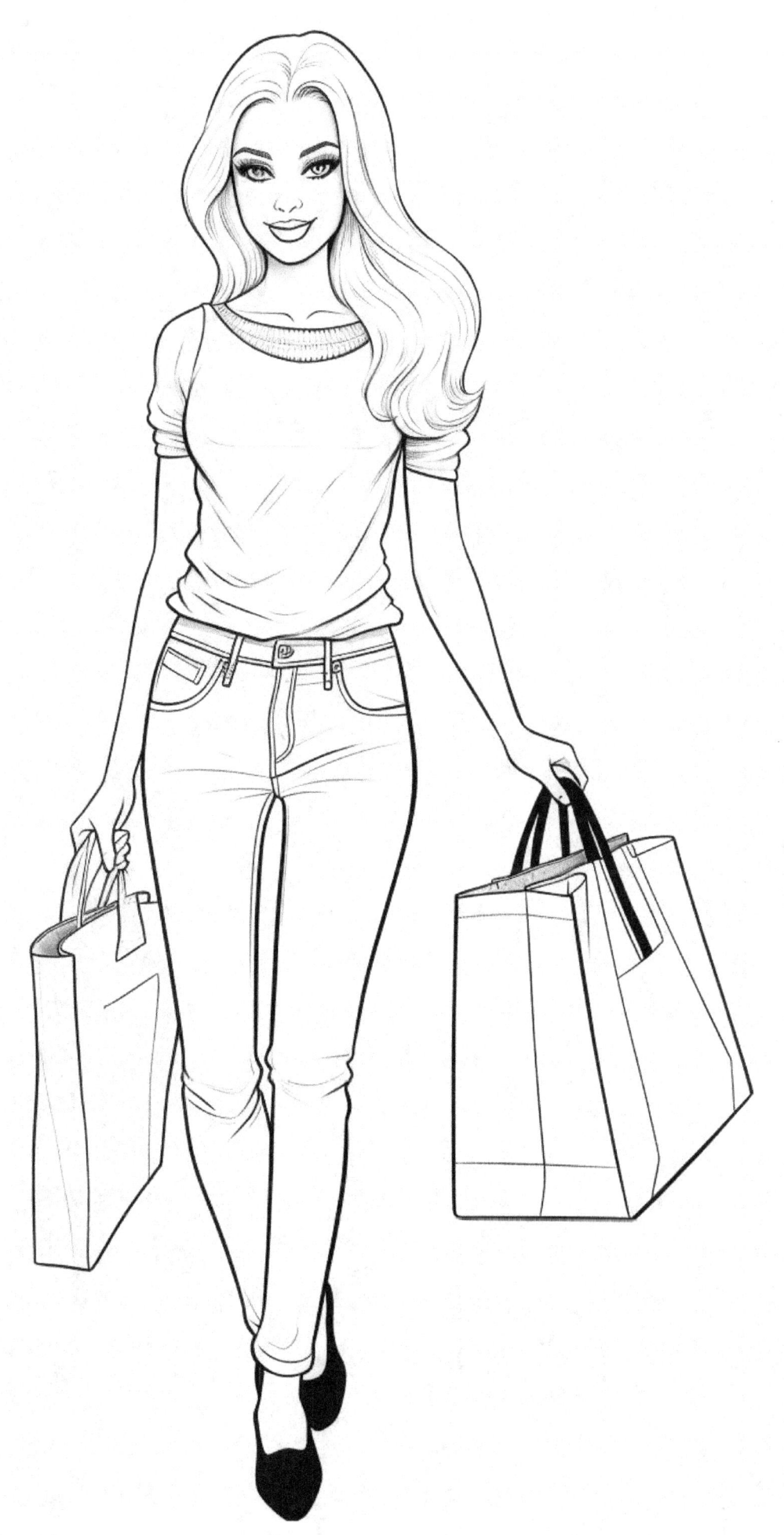

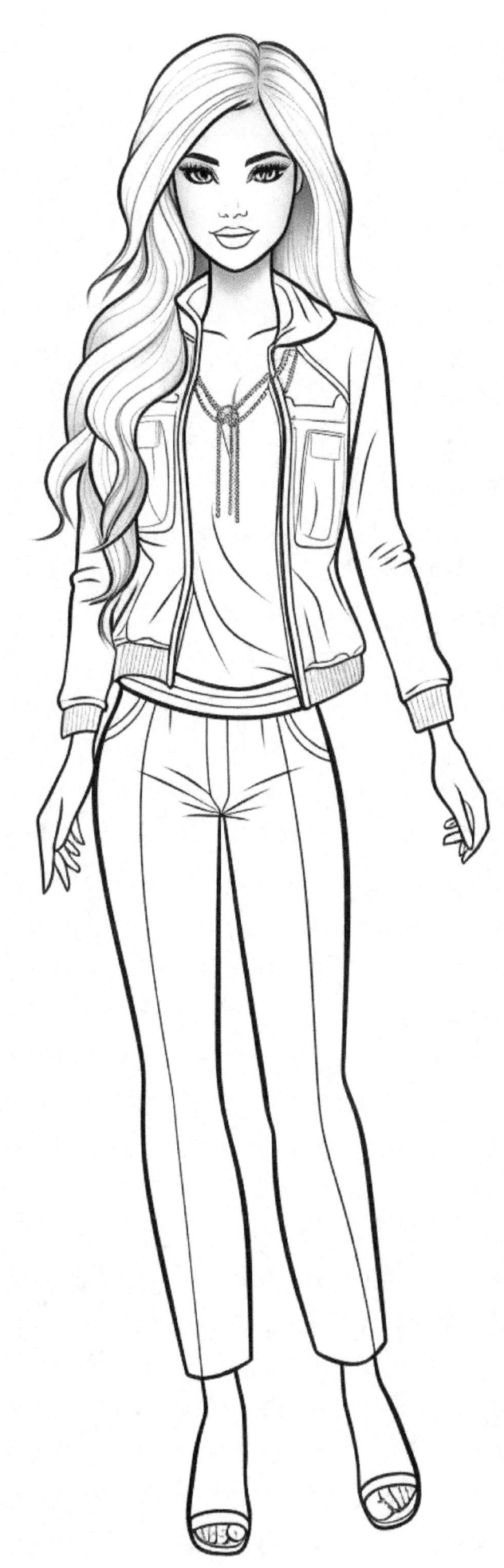

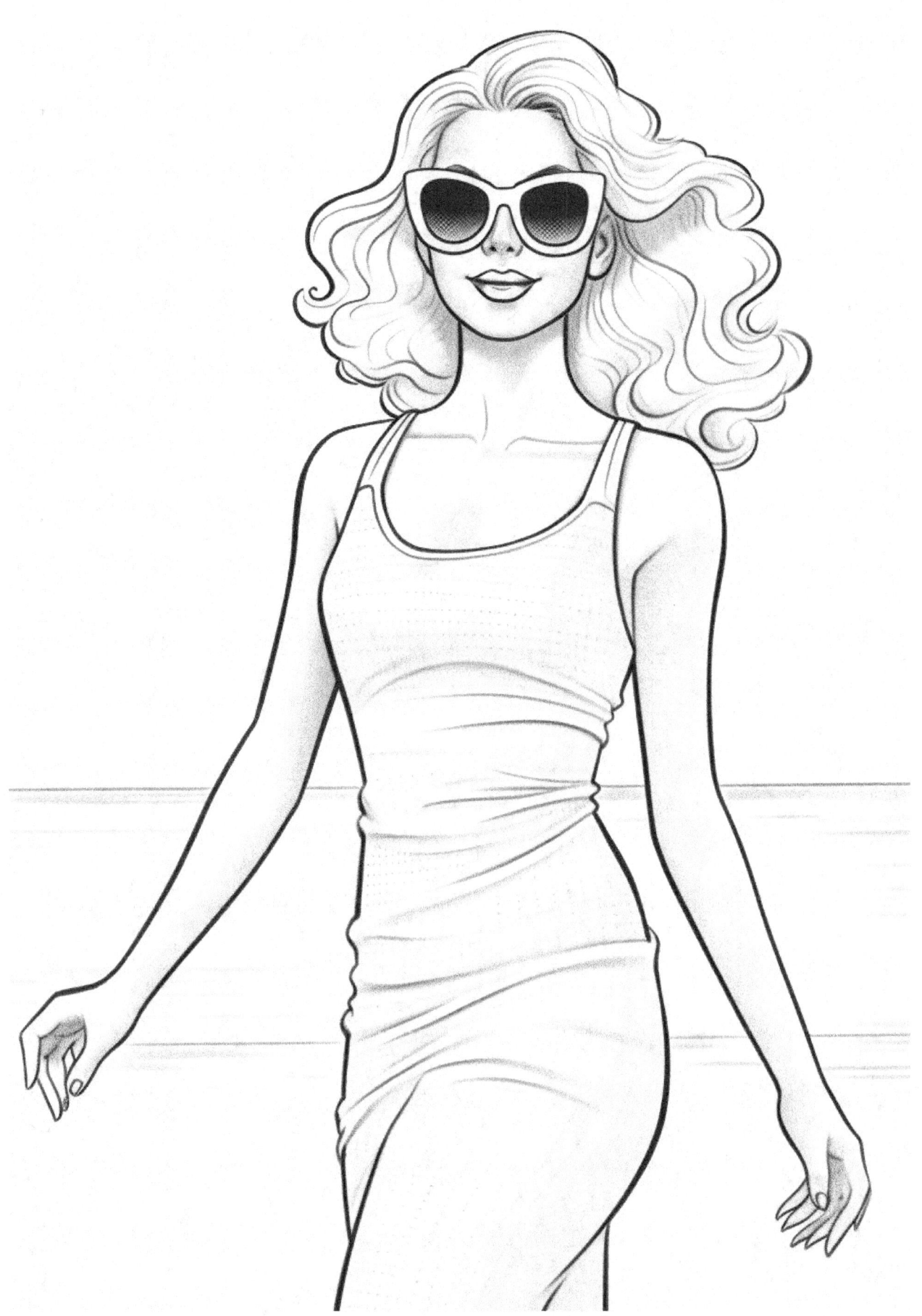

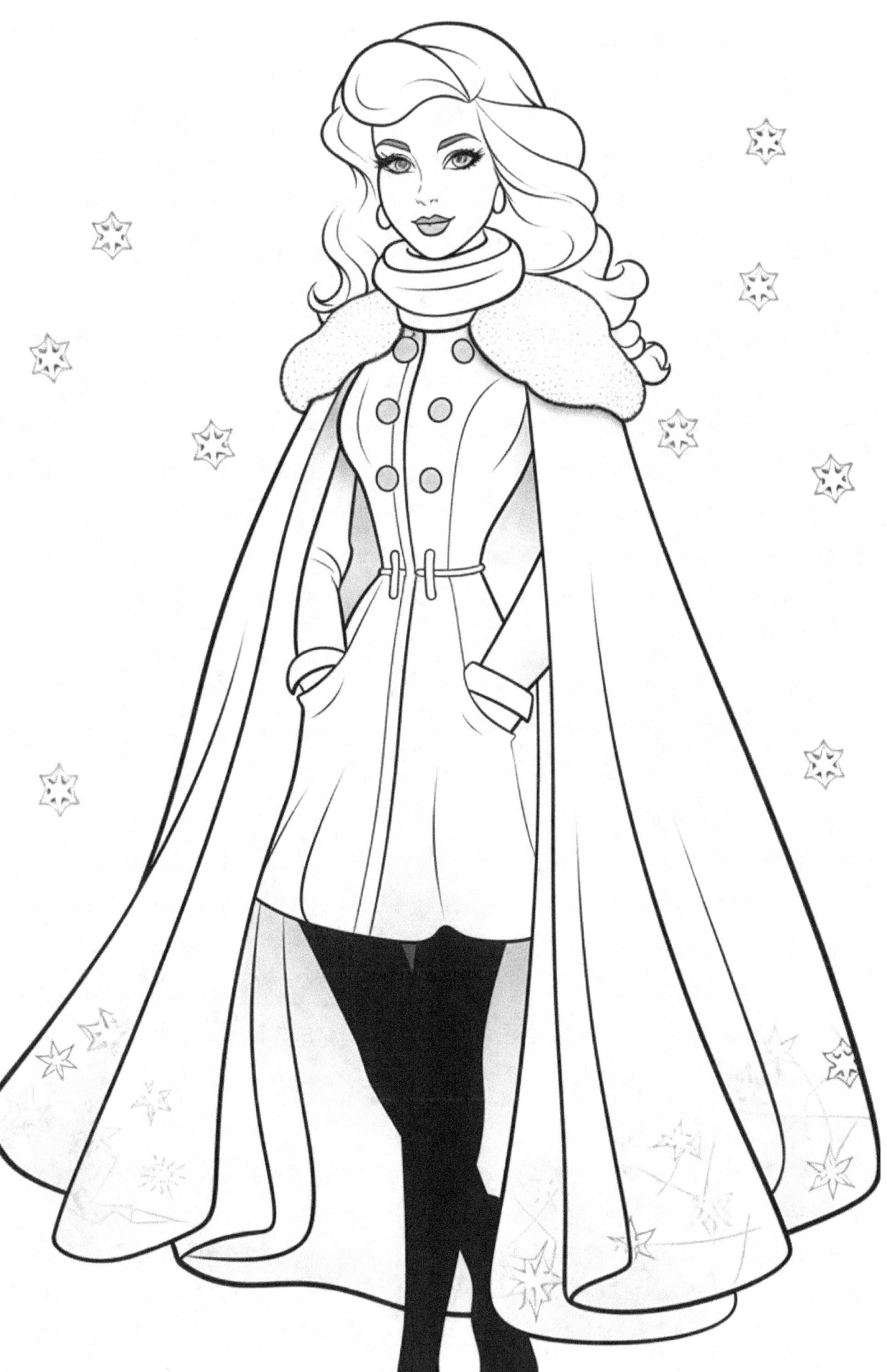

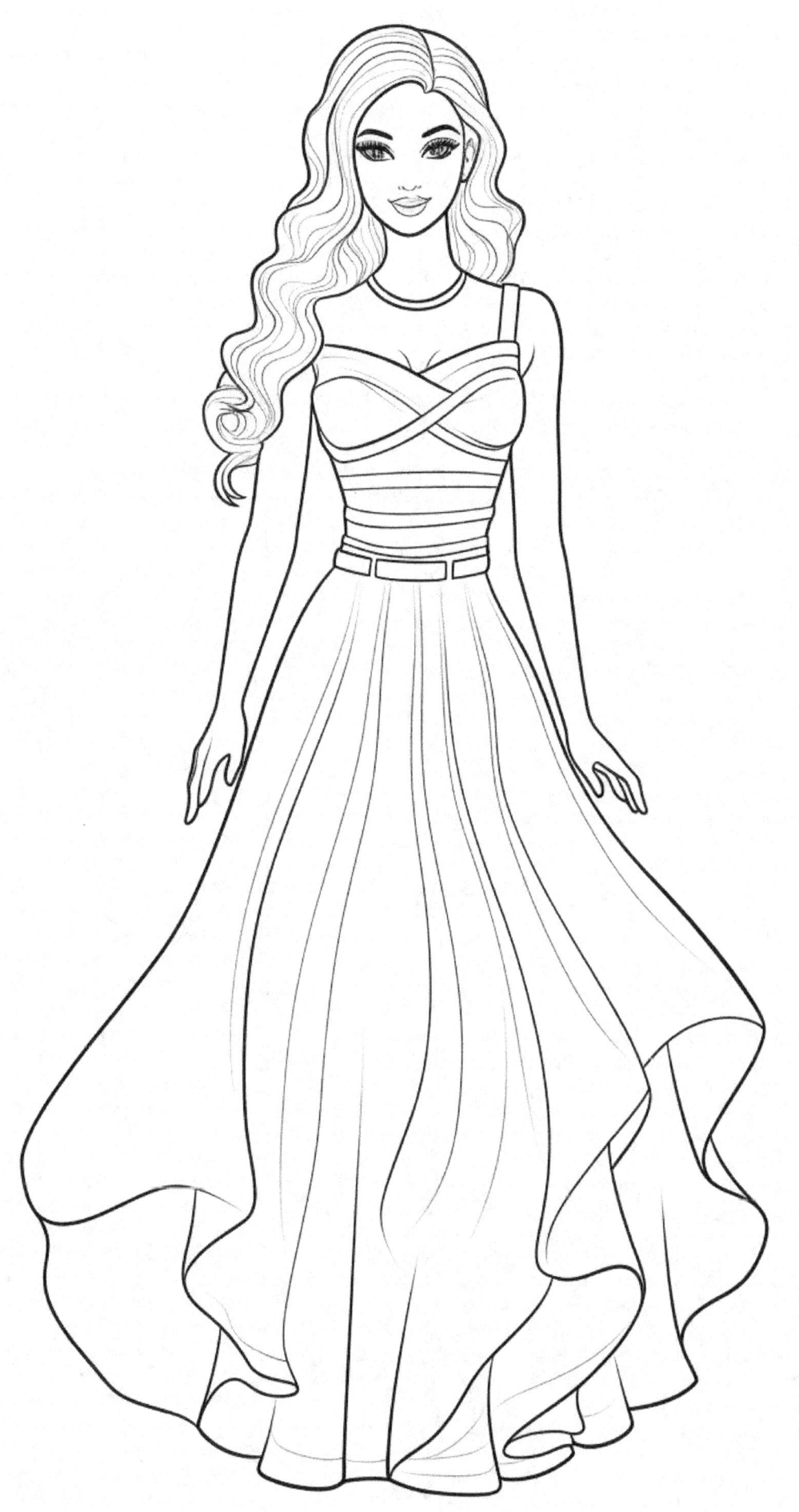

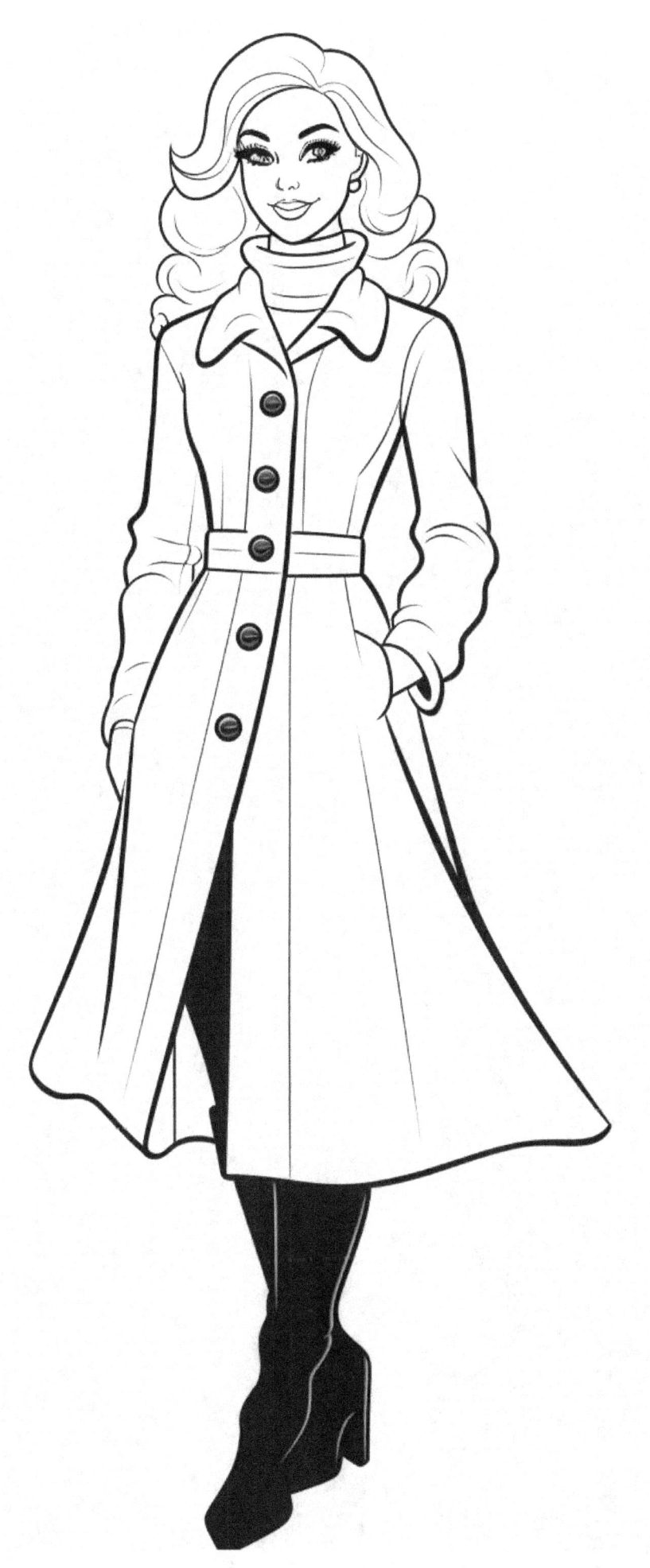

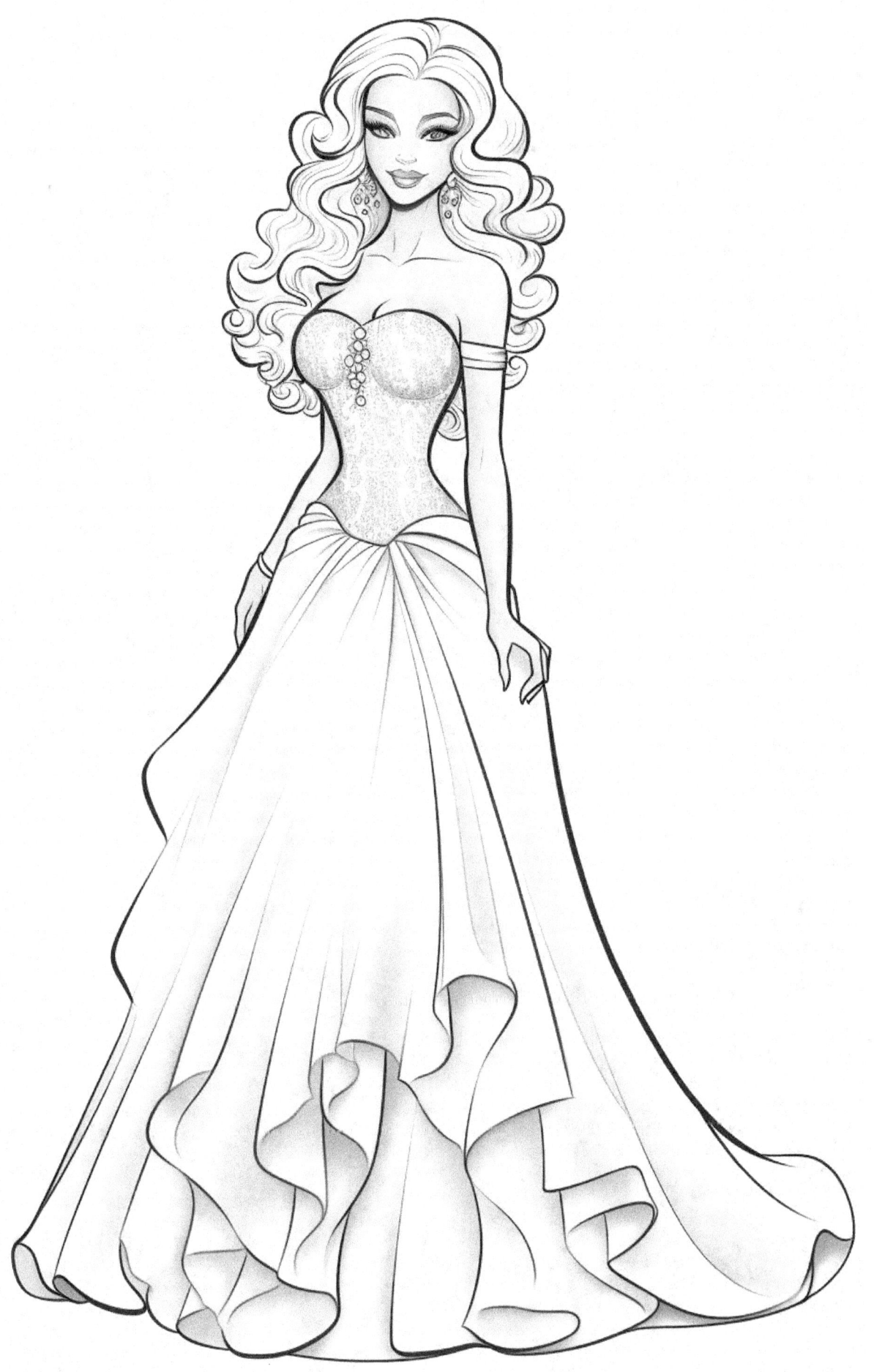

"Artificial Art" Collection
Other titles in the collection

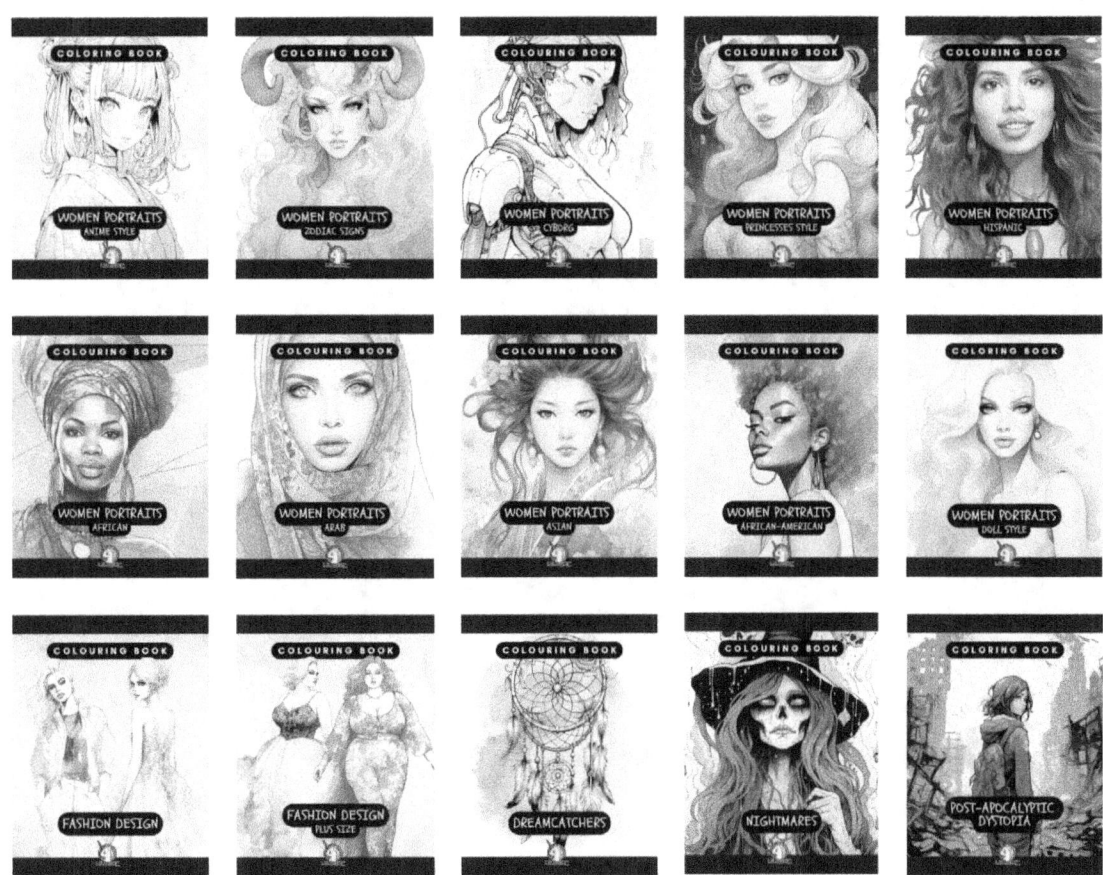

Lidia Contreras Ochando

🐦 @liconoc

📷 @lilinocbooks

www.ingramcontent.com/pod-product-compliance
Lightning Source LLC
Chambersburg PA
CBHW082212290526
45794CB00009B/3516